CHAMPLAIN AND THE CHAMPLAIN SOCIETY

*An Early Expedition
into Documentary Publishing*

Figure 1. Byron Edmund Walker. Founder and President of The Champlain Society (1905–24). Photo taken in 1908 when he served as Commissioner on the National Battlefields Commission

CHAMPLAIN AND THE CHAMPLAIN SOCIETY

*An Early Expedition
into Documentary Publishing*

Occasional Papers
Number 3

Conrad E. Heidenreich

General Editor, Champlain Society
Roger Hall

Toronto
Published by The Champlain Society, 2006

Copyright © 2006 by The Champlain Society

All rights reserved. No part of this work may be reproduced in any form without the prior permission in writing of the publisher, except by a reviewer who wishes to quote brief passages in connection with a review written for inclusion in a magazine or newspaper.

Library and Archives Canada Cataloguing in Publication

Heidenreich, Conrad E., 1936-
Champlain and the Champlain Society : an early expedition into documentary publishing / Conrad E. Heidenreich.

(Occasional papers ; no. 3)
ISBN 0-9689317-4-X / 978-0-9689317-4-5

1. Champlain Society—Publishing—History. 2. Champlain, Samuel de, 1567-1635. 3. Walker, Edmund, Sir, 1848-1924. 4. Biggar, Henry Percival, 1872-1938. I. Champlain Society II. Title. III. Series: Occasional papers (Champlain Society); no. 3.

FC152.H44 2006   971.01'13092   C2006-905186-0

Typesetting and print production by Becker Associates, Toronto
Cover design by Adam Becker
Cover: "Champlain's Picture Plan of the Abitation de Quebec", Plate IV, taken from H. P. Biggar, ed., *The Works of Samuel Champlain,* Volume II, Toronto, The Champlain Society, 1925, p. 39. (see Legend on page vi)
Printed and bound in Canada by Marquis, Quebec

The Champlain Society
Box 507, Station Q
Toronto, Ontario M4T 2M5
Canada

Printed on acid-free paper

Dedication

This monograph is dedicated to all those editors, translators and administrators who worked on the Champlain Society edition of
The Works of Samuel de Champlain

Sir Edmund Walker
(1848-1924)
President of the Canadian Bank of Commerce
President, The Champlain Society, 1905-24

Henry Percival Biggar
(1872-1938)
Chief Archivist for Canada in Europe

John Home Cameron
(c.1865-1944)
Professor of French, University of Toronto

William Francis Ganong
(1864-1941)
Professor of Botany, Smith College

Hugh Hornby Langton
(1862-1953)
Chief Librarian, University of Toronto

William Dawson LeSueur
(1840-1917)
Civil servant, Historian, Critic, Man of Letters

John Squair
(1850-1928)
Professor of French, University of Toronto

William Stewart Wallace
(1884-1970)
Chief Librarian, University of Toronto

George MacKinnon Wrong
(1860-1948)
Professor of History, University of Toronto

Julia Jarvis
(1899-1987)
Executive Secretary, The Champlain Society

Cover: "Champlain's Picture Plan of the Abitation de Quebec", Plate IV, taken from H. P. Biggar, ed., *The Works of Samuel Champlain*, Volume II, Toronto, The Champlain Society, 1925, p. 39.

Legend for *Abitation de Quebec* (from Champlain's original sketch as reproduced on cover)

A Le magazin.	logemens.	N Plattes formes, en façon de tenailles pour mettre le canon.
B Colombier.	H Logis du sieur de Champlain.	
C Corps de logis où sont nos armes, & pour loger les ouuriers.	I La porte de l'habitation, où il y a Pont-leuis.	O Iardin du sieur de Champlain.
D Autre corps de logis pour les ouuriers.	L Promenoir autour de l'habitation contenant 10. pieds de large iusques sur le bort du fossé.	P La cuisine.
E Cadran.		Q Place deuant l'habitation sur le bort de la riuiere.
F Autre corps de logis où est la forge, & artisans logés.	M Fossés tout autour de l'habitation.	R La grande riuiere de sainct Lorens.
G Galleries tout autour des		

English translation from Biggar, except for N, which he omitted.

A The Warehouse.
B Pigeon loft.
C Detached Building where we keep our arms and for Lodging our Workmen.
D Another Detached Building for the Workmen.
E Sun-dial.
F Another Detached Building where is the Smithy and where the Workmen are Lodged.
G Galleries all around the Lodgings.

H The Sieur de Champlain's Lodgings.
I The door of the Settlement with a Draw-bridge.
L Promenade around the Settlement ten feet in width to the edge of the Moat.
M Moat the whole way around the Settlement.

[N Platforms in the style of tenailles for placing the cannon.]
O The Sieur de Champlain's Garden.
P The Kitchen.
Q Space in front of the Settlement on the Shore of the River.
R The great River St. Lawrence.

CONTENTS

Champlain and the Champlain Society: An Early Expedition into Documentary Publishing

INTRODUCTION 1

BYRON EDMUND WALKER AND THE ORIGIN OF THE CHAMPLAIN SOCIETY 5
    Byron Edmund Walker 5
    Founding the Champlain Society, 1905 to 1906 14
    Conception of the Champlain Project 21

EDITING *THE WORKS OF SAMUEL DE CHAMPLAIN*, 1905-1939. 35
    Editing the First Volume, 1905 to 1922 35
    Editing the Later Volumes, 1922 to 1936 55
        Volume II, 1919 to 1925 55
        Volume III, 1924 to 1930 67
        Volume IV, 1930 to 1932 73
        Volume V and VI, 1932 to 1936 77
    Winding up the Project, 1936 to 1939 84

CONCLUDING REMARKS. 89

APPENDICES
    I.   Byron E. Walker, "Address," *The Canadian Club, Ottawa,*
          February 4, 1904. 95
    II. Charles W. Colby, "Patriotism and History," *Proceedings of the*
          Canadian Club, Toronto, March 6th, 1905 101
    III. Memo by Mr. Joseph-Edmond Roy to Sir Wilfrid Laurier outlining a
          Proposed edition of Champlain's *Works*, November 21, 1907 108
    IV. Champlain's Original Works, Reprints and Translations 110
    V. Letter by Henry Percival Biggar to George Wrong, April 15, 1911 115
    VI. Letter by Sir George Garneau to W.S. Wallace, September 29, 1938 118

Tables

1. Relationship between the Laverdière edition and the Champlain Society edition 119
2 a. Publications accepted, in progress, printed and cancelled, 1906-1910 120
2 b. Publications accepted, in progress, printed and cancelled, 1911-1922 121
2 c. Publications accepted, in progress, printed and cancelled, 1923-1937 123
2 d. Publications accepted, in progress, printed and cancelled, 1938-1949 125
3 a. Costs of Champlain Society volumes, 1907-1937 127
3 b. Costs of Champlain Society volumes, 1938-1948 128
4. Champlain Society financial data, 1905-1938 129

Illustrations

1. Byron Edmund Walker, 1848-1924. (Photo owned by author) ii
2. George MacKinnon Wrong, 1860-1948. (Courtesy, University of Toronto Archives, Accession # A78-0041/024 (18)) 16
3. Henry Percival Biggar, 1872-1938. (Courtesy, University of Toronto Archives, Accession # A73-0026/029(17)) 22
4. Hugh Hornby Langton, 1862-1953. (Photo of portrait by Sir Wyly Grier, used with permission of the University of Toronto Library) .. 28
5. William Francis Ganong, 1864-1941. (Courtesy, New Brunswick Museum, Saint John, N.B., Accession # 5530) 30
6. William Dawson LeSueur, 1840-1917. (Courtesy, Royal Society of Canada) 31
7. Champlain's map *le grand sautl st louis*, from: *Les Voyages...* (Jean Berjon: Paris, 1613): 293. (Courtesy, Library and Archives of Canada, Neg. # NL 15316) 38
8. Ganong's sketch map Plate VII, covering the same area as Figure 7, from *The Works of Samuel de Champlain*, vol. 2 (The Champlain Society: Toronto, 1925): 185. (Courtesy, The Champlain Society) ... 39
9. John Home Cameron, c. 1865–1944. (Courtesy, University of Toronto Archives, Accession # LE 3T723 F77- facing p. 184) 43
10. John Squair, 1850-1928. (Courtesy, University of Toronto Archives, Accession # A78-0041/021 (021)) 57

11. William Stewart Wallace, 1884-1970. (Courtesy, University of Toronto Archives, Accession # A78-0041/22 (67) 58
12. Julia Jarvis, 1899-1987. (Courtesy, Thomas Fisher Rare Book Library, University of Toronto, MS Coll. 284. Accession # F 3063).......... 60
13. Samuel de Champlain, *Les Voyages de la nouvelle France... Traitté de La Marine* (Paris: Louis Sevestre, 1632): 36...................... 80
14. Samuel de Champlain, *Les Voyages de la nouvelle France... Traitté de La Marine* (Paris: Louis Sevestre, 1632): 37 81
15. J. Home Cameron's editorial comments on the *Traitté de La Marine*, from: *Œuvres de Champlain*, tome 6 (Québec, 1870): 38, edited by C.-H. Laverdière. (Courtesy, Thomas Fisher Rare Book Library, University of Toronto, MS Coll. 50, fol. 12, p.38. Accession # F 3061) 82
16. J. Home Cameron's editorial comments on the *Traitté de La Marine*, from: *Œuvres de Champlain*, tome 6 (Québec, 1870): 39, edited by C.-H. Laverdière. (Courtesy, Thomas Fisher Rare Book Library, University of Toronto, MS Coll 50, fol. 12, p. 39. Accession # F 3062) 83

INTRODUCTION

> The object of The Champlain Society shall be the editing and publication of works pertaining to Canada. These publications will be in such a style as to make the volumes a pleasure to book-lovers. *Constitution of the Champlain Society, 1905.*

Founded in 1905, by the close of 2005 the Society had published 101 books and was the oldest society of its kind in Canada. It seems therefore appropriate to mark its centenary through the publication of a short monograph related to the most important event in its early history.

There are three short "sketches" of the history of The Champlain Society, the last of which was updated in 1981.[1] These sketches could be revised again but it seems preferable that the overall major topic receive a much more thorough treatment at some future time. Further published sources on the early history of the Society are the reminiscences of Miss Julia Jarvis, who was executive secretary from 1924 to 1959.[2] Some caution must be exercised with these recollections, as they are in places at variance with the documentary record. The vast bulk of material relating to the Society is in the Thomas Fisher Rare Book Library at the University of Toronto.[3] In spite of a good finding aid, this collection of letters, ledgers and minutes of meetings needs a great deal of patience and perseverance to investigate. Also of importance are the papers of Sir Edmund Walker, the founder of the Society, especially his correspondence.[4]

Rather than making further revisions of existing histories, it was determined to be more useful on this anniversary of the Society's establishment to study the circumstances surrounding that founding and the immediate involvement in the collating, editing

---

1   William Stewart Wallace, *A Sketch of the History of the Champlain Society* (Toronto: The Champlain Society, 1937). An update was published by Wallace in 1957 and another update by the historian Charles P. Stacey in 1981, all under the same title. The latter is the longest of the three *Sketches* at twelve pages.
2   Julia Jarvis, "Speech given on May 17, 1978, Part 1," *The Champlain Society, 83rd Annual Report* (Toronto, 1990): [9–11]; "Speech, Part 2," *84th Annual Report* (1991): 9–11; and "Speech, Part 3," *85th Annual Report* (1992): 13–16.
3   Thomas Fisher Rare Book Library, MS Collection 50, Champlain Society Papers. A finding aid can be reached on the Internet at: <http://www.library.utoronto.ca/fisher/findaids/champlain.pdf>. Henceforth: MS Coll. 50.
4   Thomas Fisher Rare Book Library, MS Collection 1, Walker Papers. Henceforth: MS Coll. 1.

and publication of the *Works of Samuel de Champlain* to coincide with the Québec Tercentenary in 1908. This monumental project began in 1905, did not end until 1939 and remains to date the Society's greatest single undertaking. At the same time as the Champlain material was being edited, the Society was engaged in editing and publishing books in its regular series, beginning with Lescarbot's *Histoire de la Nouvelle France*. It was probably ill advised to begin with such an ambitious publication programme since none of the original participants except Henry Percival Biggar had much experience in editing and publishing bilingual documents. In fact the Champlain project was almost to sink the Society financially and create hard feelings among some of its editors and members of the executive. The Champlain project provides however, an intimate view into the early workings of the Society: the idealism behind its founding; the chronic shortages of funding; the diplomacy (and sometimes lack of it) that was exercised in relations with the academic editors; personality conflicts; the constant pressure by the executive and Council on the editors who had busy lives outside the Society, to meet editing and publication deadlines; the difficulties of dealing with a press and a chief editor who were in England; the painfully slow communications between executive, editors and press that were almost entirely by surface mail; interruptions caused by World War I that led to delays in publication and sharp rises in the price of almost everything; all these factors and more characterized the project. When the final volume ran off the press in 1936 the group of editors involved in the Champlain project had produced a fitting monument to the Québec Tercentenary. It is our hope that most of the themes that run through this project have been adequately explored to give a glimpse into the early workings of our Society and the nature of documentary editing.

In order to understand the times and circumstances under which the Society was founded this monograph begins with a short biography of Sir Edmund Walker.[5] A self made man, by profession a banker; he reorganized and expanded the Canadian Bank of Commerce from modest Ontario origins into a national bank. His passion however was for literature, history, palaeontology and the arts. His love for Canada and the sense of duty he felt to further its development drove him to create educational and cultural institutions for the nation's citizens. Of these institutions, The Champlain Society was one he cherished the most.

---

5 A complete study of Walker has yet to be written. The best short biography is by David Kimmel, "Walker, Sir Byron Edmund," *Dictionary of Canadian Biography: Volume 15, 1921-1930* (Toronto: University of Toronto Press, 2005). The only book length study, written by George P. de T. Glazebrook, *Sir Edmund Walker* (London: Oxford University Press, 1933) was commissioned by Walker's family. The "Foreword" by Sir Robert Falconer, a close personal friend of Sir Edmund's, is excellent. A good, but almost inaccessible study is by Barbara R. Marshall, "Sir Edmund Walker, Servant of Canada" (Master's Thesis, Department of History, University of British Columbia, Vancouver, 1971). Marshall's thesis has the most complete references to Walker's family and youth.

I would like to thank my son Robert and my wife Nancy for their help in reading parts of the Walker Papers in order to get an understanding of Sir Edmund's sense of patriotism, views of history and education. Robert researched the larger part on Edmund Walker in the next section of this monograph. As our research progressed we came across evidence of a number of other projects in which Walker was involved in his capacity as president of The Champlain Society, such as the National Battlefields Commission, the Québec Tercentenary and the Champlain Monument in Orillia, Ontario. Unfortunately space and time do not permit a closer look into activities such as these that took place during the time Champlain's *Works* were being edited.

I would also like to thank the librarians and archivists at the Thomas Fisher Rare Book Library and the University of Toronto Archives for their friendly and exceptional service. I have never met a better-informed and efficient group of professionals who made every visit productive and a pleasure. I would also like to thank the New Brunswick Museum for making the photograph of William F. Ganong available to me.

Conrad Edmund Heidenreich
De Grassi Point, Ontario
June 22, 2006

BYRON EDMUND WALKER AND THE ORIGIN OF THE CHAMPLAIN SOCIETY

Not to go on learning is fatal / The world is intensely interesting / No end to wealth of facts and ideas / Every moment throbs with meaning / Knowledge is the supreme thing / A noble curiosity is the greatest gift to man. *Sir Edmund Walker, 1922.*[1]

BYRON EDMUND WALKER

In order to trace the genesis of The Champlain Society it is necessary and interesting to examine the background and personal principles that drove its founder and first president, Byron Edmund Walker,[2] to establish what remains Canada's oldest historical society.

Edmund Walker's grandfather, Thomas Walker (1783–1857), was an educated man who had been a maker of watchcases in London, England. Between 1828 and 1830 his wife Isabella and four of their children had died. About the same time Thomas was facing the loss of his business through the beginnings of mechanized watch making. These circumstances prompted him in 1834 to seek a healthier and more prosperous environment in Canada with four of his remaining children. A married daughter remained in England. Grandfather Walker settled on a 100 acre farm, on Lot 9 along the west side of the road to Hamilton on the northern outskirts of the town of Caledonia, Seneca Township, Ontario. Thomas Walker had brought with him a small library, "a few good pictures," and enough money to exist as a man "of comfortable means."[3] Edmund Walker's father, Alfred Edmund, was the seventh of Thomas and Isabella's nine children. Alfred was a person of delicate health, unsuited to farming but with an enquiring mind and a love for learning. He was a fine artist, especially with watercolours and developed, through reading and his wanderings along the Grand

---

1   MS Coll. 1, box 34 A, fol. 16, "Notes on an address on banking, 14 December 1922."
2   Byron Edmund Walker usually signed his full name, or B.E. Walker, or simply B.E.W. His wife and close relatives often called him "Ned" or Edmund. When George V knighted him in 1910, in keeping with the rules of knighthood he had to choose one of his given names and chose to be called Sir Edmund. Unless quoting directly from a document, in this essay he will be called Edmund Walker.
3   Ibid., box 41, item 41:23. Bowman to Harold Walker, 20 May 1924. Letter written by Mrs. Edith (Walker) Bowman to her nephew Harold Walker (Sir Edmund's youngest child) expressing her condolences to Harold on his father's death, 27 March 1924.

River and Niagara Escarpment a strong interest in natural science, especially geology and fossils. In 1845 he married Fanny Murton, a neighbour from Caledonia, fifth born of fifteen children, who had emigrated to Canada with her family in 1832. Alfred and Fanny had nine children of whom Edmund, born in 1848, was the second oldest. In 1852 Alfred left his father's farm with his growing family and moved to Hamilton, where he became a clerk and bookkeeper. Soon after his arrival, Alfred joined The Hamilton Scientific Association and later became president of its geological section. He was also an abolitionist who used his artistic talents to good effect in 1860–61 by producing lithographs, requested by Hamilton newspapers, of American sheriffs who had entered Canada to apprehend escaped slaves. These pictures were published to alert Hamilton citizens of the American's unwanted presence.[4] Edmund's youngest sister Edith Bowman described their mother and father in the following terms:

> [Mother was] a woman of dominant type, resourceful, unselfish and of considerable executive ability, and without whose courageous and skilful hand, our little family barque would never have reached smooth waters. [Father] was of a gentle nature and fine mind.[5]

In Hamilton, young Edmund, aged four, entered a private junior school owned and operated by his maternal grandmother Mary Wenn Murton (*née* Coleman), a lady of considerable learning, who was fluent in French and Italian and "the only woman west of Toronto who could play the harpsichord."[6] A few years later he started at the Hamilton Central School where he ended his formal education with grade six. While in his last year at school he met his future wife Mary ("Minnie") Alexander who was three years his junior. The two had similar interests that drew them together, especially literature, poetry, engravings and sketching. As a youth, with the first money he earned he began a subscription to Bartlett's *Canada* at 25 cents a month. Later he had all the instalments bound into a volume for his growing library.[7] The first book he ever purchased was *The Life of Mahomet*.[8] He was fond of reading Victorian novels and collecting fossils with his father.

---

4   MS Coll. 1, box 25, Walker to Riddell, 26 July 1920. Walker wrote to the Hon. Walter A. Riddell congratulating him on his article, "The Slave in Upper Canada," *Journal of Negro History* (vol. 4, no. 4, 1919): 372–95. In the letter he mentioned his father's role in publicizing the presence of American sheriffs in Hamilton in the case of the escaped slave John Anderson whom the Queen's Bench, Toronto, had ordered extradition to Missouri on December 15, 1860. After considerable public pressure Chief Justice William Draper overturned this decision on February 16, 1861. Between 1854 and 1860 Anderson had worked in Caledonia and Hamilton. It is possible that the Walker family knew him.
5   Ibid., box 41, item 41: 23. Bowman to Harold Walker, 20 May 1924.
6   Ibid.
7   Ibid., box 21, Walker to Morris, 20 January 1917. The bound set of Bartlett's *Canadian Scenery* was still in Sir Edmund's library when he died in 1924.
8   Ibid., box 41, fol. 41:4. In his autobiographical notes Walker wrote that he was about 14 years of age when he bought the book. The book was no longer in his library when he died.

A frail constitution prevented Edmund from pursuing studies at the Normal School in Toronto toward the teaching career that his parents thought suited him.[9] Instead, in August 1861, he entered the business world at the age of twelve years and ten months in the currency exchange office of his uncle, John W. Murton, in Hamilton. Soon after Edmund's arrival at the exchange his uncle discovered that his nephew had an extraordinary eye and memory for fine engravings, with the result that Edmund quickly became "a recognized expert in counterfeit money."[10] In September 1868, while his uncle was in Europe, Edmund saved the exchange office from financial ruin through a series of shrewd moves when the bank of Upper Canada failed. Years later he still recalled the event as "the greatest day in my life." [11]

One might think that the world of finance would serve to limit a child's imagination and creative development at such an impressionable age, but by his early teens the Walker household had already transformed Edmund into an individual with very broad interests. At the Golden Jubilee Dinner in 1918, commemorating his 50th year at the Canadian Bank of Commerce, Walker gave a rare public glimpse into his childhood and the atmosphere with which his parents had tried to surround him:

> Whatever qualities I may possess, apart from mere industry, I owe to my father. At home I never heard money talked about, except perhaps the need of it, which was always the case. We instead talked about flowers, music, fossils, science, a new poem or novel—nothing very learned or difficult. I was taught to appreciate that the truth concerning Nature was the divine thing, and that we must learn it so far as it is possible. I remember the comfort that Darwin's books were to my father.[12]

Darwin's writings made a great intellectual impact on the Walker family. Edmund Walker's oldest son, Edmund Murton Walker, recalled the following:

> Both Grandfather [Alfred Edmund] and Father [Byron Edmund] were interested in natural history in a broad sense, and Father told me years later with what satisfaction they read Darwin's *Origin of the Species* when it first appeared. They devoured it eagerly and accepted it with enthusiasm, for it gave them a logical explanation of much that was hinted at in their studies of fossils. By the time I was old enough to understand what was meant by evolution I was ready to accept it, although my ideas of the process were still vague and very limited.[13]

---

9   Ibid., box 43, fol. 7. In his notes Walker wrote that the family physician had forbidden sending him to a school away from home due to his frail health.
10 [Canadian Bank of Commerce]. *Jubilee of Sir Edmund Walker, C.V.O., LL.D., C.C.L., 1868–1918* [Toronto, 1918] 24.
11 Ibid., 25.
12 Ibid., 35.
13 Edmund M. Walker, "Autobiographical Sketch," in *Centennial of Entomology in Canada, 1863–1963, A Tribute to Edmund M. Walker*, ed. Glenn B. Wiggins (Toronto: University of Toronto Press, 1966). Edmund M. Walker was appointed to the Zoology Department at the University of Toronto in 1906 and was chair from 1931 until he retired in 1948. He was widely known as an authority on insects, especially the *Orthoptera* (grasshoppers and crickets) and the *Odonata* (dragonflies).

Like his father, Edmund Murton spent a great deal of time with his grandfather Alfred Edmund on hikes in the Hamilton area examining fossils, plants, animals and insects.

Walker was born with a remarkable memory and the ability for structured thinking, or, as he put it, "…a good memory and systematic hooks in my mind on which to hang individual facts as learned."[14] He had a natural curiosity about his surroundings; a strong imagination and a powerful drive to succeed in the tasks he set for himself or others set for him. His father Alfred, explored nature, history, literature, art and music with his son and recognized these qualities very early. It was his father who gently guided him in an uncomplicated and thought provoking manner into systematic observation, thinking and recording. With his natural gifts and his father's tutelage young Edmund developed an interest in continuous learning. In fact, he was largely self-taught—improving himself through observation of his surroundings, through the systematic study of whatever he was reading, through observing other people and through innovative action. The broad intellectual background provided by his family and his desire for learning was to be crucial to Walker's later activities when they were united with his developing organizational abilities, his sense of patriotism and the sense of duty he felt toward the emerging Canadian nation.

Walker's experiences in the exchange office and later with the Canadian Bank of Commerce taught him leadership and organizational skills. By his late teens he had developed a sense of self-confidence through his natural abilities and the confidence others had shown in his judgments and work habits. He was modest rather than ambitious; what got him ahead in the business world were his abilities, and his complete dedication, often in an innovative manner, to accomplish anything he was asked to do or chose to do. He would not take on an obligation, no matter how great or small, if he felt he could not make a major commitment and contribution. From his youth onward, probably through his experiences with his father, he became what he called a "liberal thinker." Remarkable for his time and station he was relatively free of race prejudice. On several occasions he urged that Canada accept more Asian and Black immigrants. On at least one occasion he castigated "the white race" for their prejudice against Jews and Asians, and blamed the "cruelty of all dominant races" for the "position of blacks in human society."[15] Walker, who had a subscription to the *Journal of Negro History* published by the Washington-based "Association for the Study of Negro Life and History," was placed on their Executive Council in 1917 because they knew him to be "a friend of the man far down and…interested in the propagation of the truth."[16] Although

---

14   *Jubilee of Sir Edmund Walker*: 35.
15   MS Coll, 1, box 34A, fol. 14, Notes of speech for *The Canadian Observer* (Toronto) 13 December 1915.
16   MS Coll. 1, box 57, fol. "September," and "October." Woodson to Walker, 8 September 1917 and 20 October 1917. Dr. Woodson founded the Association and *Journal of Negro History*, now called the *Journal of African American History*, in 1916.

he believed in a strong independent Canada, he also valued Canada's connections to the British Empire. Later in life, he felt that due to his influential position as a banker he should never join a political party. Instead he gave advice to both the Liberal and Conservative governments on matters that he could support, but was not adverse to oppose either of them if he felt Canada's interests as he saw them, were threatened. As a young man he had tried both the Anglican and Unitarian Churches, but never became a regular "churchgoer." After he married Mary Alexander in 1874, a Presbyterian, they became members of St. Andrews Presbyterian Church on King Street, Toronto. He joined for love of his wife and not out of any deep religious feeling. In fact, upon joining St. Andrew's, he told the minister that he "could not accept the doctrine of the divinity of Christ."[17] With the death of his wife in 1923 he stopped going to church. During his long association with educational institutions, particularly with the University of Toronto, he became known as an original thinker and a defender of academic freedom, even on the occasions when he strongly disagreed with particular opinions or actions. He expressed the view that progress in all endeavours is dependent on uncensored scientific, historical and philosophical inquiry. Religious or political dogma, economic theory, or the channeling of the thought process that can come from schooling did not seem to influence him. He read widely, listened to those whom he respected, thought things through and finally acted on his own judgments. The few, who knew him well, stated that the only person whom he trusted completely and confided in was his wife.

Throughout his life, Walker continued adding to his knowledge in areas that interested him outside banking. In 1873, five years after he had joined the Canadian Bank of Commerce he was sent to New York as a junior agent. This two-year sojourn began his introduction to the world of art galleries, museums and literary circles. When he later returned to Yonkers, New York in 1881, this time for five years as joint agent for the Canadian Bank of Commerce, he and his wife Mary took the opportunity to immerse themselves in the cultural opportunities that surrounded them. It was at this time that he broadened his knowledge of art and developed a life-long interest in Japanese woodblock prints, Robert Browning and John Ruskin.

By the time he died in 1924, Walker had an enormous library. A partial reconstruction of the contents of that library lists 1100 titles. In order of importance to him judged by the number of titles of the subjects covered are: "literature, art, poetry, biography, Canadian history, government and politics, travel and exploration."[18] This inventory does not include his collection of some 500 geological books, journals, pamphlets and "several thousand" fossil specimens that he had collected and donated to the University

---

17   Ibid., box 41, item 41:4. "Autobiographical notes."
18   This information was supplied by Ms Andrea Rotundo (e-mail, March 7, 2006) who is working on Sir Edmund's library for a practicum component in the Collaborative Program in Book History and Print Culture at the U. of T. She is a doctoral student in that program.

of Toronto in 1904. The fossils formed the beginning of the collection in the Royal Ontario Museum.[19] His collection of engraving and prints that began modestly with his youthful purchases of Bartlett's *Canadian Scenery* also grew. In 1926, his family donated his collection of about 400 prints, among them works by Whistler, Millet, Rembrandt, Dürer and Gagnon, to the Art Gallery of Ontario.[20] The same year his collection of 1,100 Japanese woodblock prints, one of the largest known private collections, was given to the Royal Ontario Museum. Charles T. Currelly, who had worked with Walker on founding the ROM and became its first director, wrote that Walker had intended the collection "for the people of Ontario" which is why it demonstrates the evolution of the art-style rather than his personal taste.[21] The estate inventory from his house at 99 St. George Street, Toronto, also lists about 140 oil paintings and watercolours. His children inherited some of these pictures and the remainder were auctioned. The pictures were mainly by eighteenth and nineteenth century English, French and Dutch painters as well as Canadian painters, including works by members of "The Group of Seven," among them two oils by Tom Thomson. During his lifetime Walker had published papers on topics as diverse as banking, geology and fossils, Italian Renaissance painters and the scientific exploration of Canada. Unfortunately he never completed the manuscript for his book on Robert Browning.[22]

As a banker, this self-educated man with far ranging interests outside the business world became enormously successful and influential. Walker rose quickly through the ranks. In 1886, aged 38 years, he was appointed general manager of the Canadian Bank of Commerce, becoming its president in 1907. He served on a number of Royal Commissions, was president of the Canadian Banker's Association and Vice President of the American Banker's Association. During his time as general manager he built the Canadian Bank of Commerce from an Ontario bank with 34 branches and an office in Montréal and New York, into a national bank with 374 branches.[23] His success as a banker was to a large degree a result of his approach to management. In a short biography of Walker, Professor Charles Colby explained Walker's approach in the following terms: "The power of imagination which was one of his outstanding qualities gathered strength from association with another, which was the power of sympathy."[24]

---

19   University of Toronto Archives, B72–003/001 (59), Walker to Hoskins, 14 July 1904. Also: *University of Toronto Monthly*, "Mr. B.E. Walker's Gift to the University," vol. 5, no. 1, October 1904: 21.
20   Katherine A. Jordan, *Sir Edmund Walker, Print Collector* (Toronto: Art Gallery of Ontario, 1974).
21   Charles T. Currelly, "Sir Edmund Walker," *Bulletin of the Royal Ontario Museum of Archaeology* (University of Toronto, July, 1927): 2. David B. Waterhouse, *Images of Eighteenth Century Japan, Ukiyoe Prints from the Sir Edmund Walker Collection* (Toronto: Royal Ontario Museum, 1975).
22   MS Coll. 1, box 40. The bundle of handwritten manuscript notes is about 8 cm thick.
23   *Jubilee of Sir Edmund Walker*, 12.
24   Charles W. Colby, "Sir Edmund Walker," *The Cadeuceus* 5, no. 2 (Toronto, June, 1924): 9.

Walker wanted to ensure that the people working for his corporation were motivated, stimulated, and co-operating together as in a "complete organism." In his own words:

> No corporation is quite secure…unless there is that liberty of action in the individual, combined with cheerful observance of discipline, which causes a body of men to move together happily and enthusiastically in the daily task. If we have prospered in the bank, I am sure it is to the extent that we have created such a staff.[25]

It was his view of corporate structure that was also fundamental to Walker's sense of a nation; the belief that people make a nation, not the reverse. If a populace is intellectually well rounded through a thorough schooling system, morally centered and imbued with a sense of where their country came from and where it is going, that nation will be prosperous and nurturing. It is not surprising therefore that he considered schooling of paramount importance in the development of a civilized society. This led to his involvement with education at every level: public and private, basic and advanced, practical and abstract.

There is no question that much of what motivated and guided Walker was his love for Canada. He was a true patriot. This is absolutely clear from his speeches, his biographical statements, and the newspaper columns and obituaries written after his death. Everything he did at each stage of his life was evaluated by his perception of whether it was good for Canada. He even regarded the Bank as an instrument in the service of the public to help develop the country.[26] His political involvements at the Provincial or Federal level, whether with the Liberals or the Conservatives, were measured in terms of whether as he saw it; they were doing the right things for Canada. It was his sense of patriotism, the special relationship he had to his country that drove him to create public institutions such as The Champlain Society.

Having been born in 1848 put Walker in a position to witness the creation of Canada; indeed, the two grew up along side each other. In his address to the Canadian Club in February of 1904, Walker spoke about how he envisioned the ideal Canadian's relationship to Canada:

> We talk constantly about the size of Canada. Its vast natural resources, its immense potency in producing natural wealth, and we take credit for all this just as if we Canadians had created Canada. Instead we should remember everyday of our lives, with bowed heads, that Canada was made for us and for our heirs, and that we are merely stewards for posterity, answerable as we do well or ill by Canada. This confidence, however, as to what Canada will do *for us* is an agreeable change from the fears expressed by the doubting Thomases of the past, but it should always be accompanied by a grave and reverent sense of what we should do for Canada—a

---

25 *Jubilee of Sir Edmund Walker*, 34.
26 Sir Edmund Walker. *Banking as a Public Service*. Address delivered before the New York Bankers' Association at Buffalo (14th June 1912): 14.

very different sort of problem from what Canada should do for us.[27] [For the full speech see Appendix I]

Walker saw in Canada a land full of promise and possibility that must be developed, but only in a way that gives back to the country by creating greater opportunity through the establishment of lasting institutions. Much later in life he made this statement:

> I have always believed in Canada. I did not understand the early Imperialists, but for many years I have believed as intensely in the Empire as in Canada, and in the desirability of a better Imperial Government. I am very conscious of what it means to be born in Canada, and I can think of no privilege so great as to have founded any good or enduring thing in this country. I know the value of money, but I should rather have created one of the institutions of my country than to possess millions.[28]

The manner in which the word "patriot" is used today and to apply that meaning to Walker scarcely does justice to the nature and depth of his feelings towards the country that gave him such opportunity. Although he valued Canada's Imperial ties, Walker was originally and thoroughly a Canadian.

For Walker, personal success in life had to be measured by more than material gain. Time devoted to one's occupation should be offset by artistic, intellectual, and scientific pursuits in order to more fully develop one's character. If this were true of the individual, said Walker, why would it not be true of the nation as well? In 1910, Walker was asked to write the Dominion Day address for the Toronto newspaper *The Globe*. In this address he warned against Canadians feeling "vain and self-satisfied" with the material success achieved through the abundance of natural resources offered by this vast country. We are not, wrote Walker, living up to an obligation to create a complete nation, and not merely a prosperous one, from the material that we have been given:

> We have seen a democracy which began with almost the noblest principles ever declared in a national manifesto, and which certainly was far from believing that money was a measure of national greatness, become by too much devotion to money making a vast nation of discontented people run by a few plutocrats.[29]

These are strong words for any social critic, but the fact that they came from a bank president made them particularly forceful. Even surrounded by an industry devoted to money and money making, Walker could not stress enough the importance to a nation of intellectual and cultural development:

> When we find a man who has devoted his life to only making money, and who has not created anything worthwhile in doing so, and who cannot read books, enjoy beautiful things or

---

27   Byron Edmund Walker, *Address to The Canadian Club, Ottawa*, (February 4th, 1904): 3.
28   *Jubilee of Sir Edmund Walker*, 38.
29   Sir Edmund Walker, "Shall Canada go Money Mad," *The Globe* (July 1, 1910): 1.

indulge in sport, we know that he has thrown his precious life away. What, then, must be the fate of a nation which does not give due place to the intellectual and artistic in life.[30]

Material prosperity, of course, has its place, but in Walker's view it is not the only end to which one's industry should be directed. Material ventures are only successful insofar as they serve to establish the basis from which the true work of a nation can proceed. This goal, according to Walker, is "to build up the intellectual life of our people…Men who…are not ashamed to urge the supreme importance of character."[31] Walker was certainly such a man. Outside of his rôle as a banker he was, among other positions, a member and President of the Canadian Institute; Trustee, Toronto General Hospital; Commissioner on the National Battlefields Commission; Member of the Historical Manuscripts Commission of the National Archives; co-founder of the Canadian Society of Authors; founder of Appleby College, Oakville, Ontario; Chairman of the Board of Trustees of the National Gallery of Canada; President of the Toronto Guild of Civic Art; President of the Art Museum of Toronto (now Art Gallery of Ontario); co-founder and Chairman of the Board of Trustees of the Royal Ontario Museum; Chairman of the Board of Governors of the Toronto Conservatory of Music; Honorary President of the Mendelssohn Choir; founder and President of The Champlain Society; Honorary Japanese Consul-General; and a Trustee, a Senator, a Governor, Chairman of the Board of Governors, and Chancellor all at the University of Toronto. According to Walker's secretary, amongst all of these accomplishments, he was most proud of The Champlain Society,[32] because it is the institution which he established that most closely reflects the ideals of Canadian intellectual, scientific and cultural development that were so dear to Walker's heart and mind.

His close friend, Sir Robert Falconer, who was president of the University of Toronto at the time of Walker's death, wrote the best summary of Sir Edmund's life and character. In that summary he stated that:

> He would, I have often thought, have made a great scientist had the opportunity come to him to attend university. He has told me that he would have preferred such a career to that of a banker, but it was denied him as circumstances had led him to work for his living since he was twelve years of age.
>
> He took great pleasure in the company of men of science, and it was perfectly fitting when he was elected a fellow of the Royal Society [1911]. Though as a matter of fact he became a

---

30 Ibid.
31 Ibid.
32 MS Coll. 1, box 41, item 41:6. Eleanor Creighton. "Memorandum: Sir Edmund Walker." MS. Written by Miss Creighton at the request of Mrs Dorothy Buhler (*née* Walker), Sir Edmund's youngest daughter, after his death in 1924. Miss Creighton was Walker's private secretary from February 1903 to November 1914 and was intimately involved in doing the necessary secretarial work in establishing the Champlain Society.

member of Section II, that devoted to Archaeology, History, and Literature, he might with equal title have belonged to the Geological Section. His most obvious claim to Section II lay in the part he took in the creation of the Champlain Society for the publication of rare materials and books on Canadian history, series which are not only a credit to Canadian scholarship but are presented in distinguished style.[33]

Founding The Champlain Society

The occasion that propelled Walker towards the establishment of The Champlain Society was a long-awaited lecture by Professor Charles W. Colby, chairman of the History Department of McGill University, given to The Canadian Club in Toronto on the sixth of March 1905, entitled "Patriotism and History."[34] [See Appendix II] Colby had been invited to give the lecture in the fall of 1904 but declined because he was "too busy."[35] A date was set for March the following year, with Colby staying at Walker's residence and Walker taking the chair at the meeting.[36] In his address, Colby attempted to illustrate the nature of the relationship between the historian and the patriot, especially with reference to the development of materials for historical education. Colby stressed the importance of patriotic sentiment among the population of a prosperous and educated nation but warned against a kind of blind, unquestioning patriotic zeal, which he found undesirable. In his view it was the person who critically analyzes the records of his ancestors with the aim of producing a stronger nation who is both the true student of history and the true patriot:

> There is probably no part of the globe where national pride and enthusiasm are stronger than in the United States. Those in Canada who have observed this phenomenon and who hold it up for our emulation often speak of the part that is played in the creation of loyalists by the elementary textbook of history. The whole argument resolves itself to this: Firstly, that a somewhat militant spirit of patriotism is desirable; and, secondly, that the historical manual should be used as a means of setting forth in picturesque and convincing fashion the facts which help glorify the national past of the arguments which go to defend the national cause. Those who repeat with unction the sentiment, "our country, right or wrong," would doubtless be content to have a colored, one-sided version of the national annals presented to children in public schools through the medium of the elementary manual.[37]

To Colby the ideal historian was someone who has:

---

33 Robert A. Falconer, "Foreword," in: Glazebrook, *Sir Edmund Walker*, xiii.
34 Charles W. Colby, "Patriotism and History," *Proceedings of the Canadian Club* (Toronto, March 6, 1905): 107–116.
35 MS Coll. 1, box 6, Colby to Walker, 14 October 1904.
36 Ibid., Macklem to Walker, 5 December 1904.
37 Colby, "Patriotism and History," 108.

...so far as is humanly possible, the disinterestedness of the dead; that he should not set forth the results of his researches with a view to justifying any special cause, or even to vindicate the record of his own ancestors...Truth is the ideal—not patriotism, nor even religion.[38]

It is this ideal form of historical research that Colby found absent in the Canada of his day. After mentioning recently published learned histories of France, England, and the United States, Colby stated that, "in the case of Canada, the materials on which a good cooperative history can alone be founded do not exist."[39] Not only was there no learned history of Canada, the archival material and scholarship required to provide the substance for such a history had not even been adequately compiled. Colby continued:

Theoretically, at least, we all desire that there should be sound and learned histories of Canada. These cannot be prepared until a large number of special topics have been investigated with minute care. Owing to the present limitation of the national archives, the work of preparing good monographs is extremely difficult and costly. Therefore one must conclude that the only sound policy is to collect and arrange these original materials without recourse to which the historian will be making a large waste of his time in writing on Canadian subjects at all.[40]

Colby then went on to describe the "shining example" of the State of Wisconsin in collecting and publishing documents relative to their history but pointed specifically to Great Britain and the role played by private learned societies:

The Selden Society, the Surtees Society, the Camden Society, the Hakluyt Society, the Spottiswoode Society, the Maitland Club, the Pipe Roll Society, and a whole host of similar organizations supported by private effort.[41]

These statements in particular were sure to have caught Walker's attention. In view of his sense of obligation toward his country coupled with his desire to produce lasting intellectual and cultural institutions, this part of Colby's address awakened in him the desire to lay the foundation for a Canadian historical society. That is, a society that would provide the framework of materials necessary to produce that sound and learned history of which Colby had spoken in order to allow his country to develop into the nation he believed it should become. Colby concluded:

Those who love their country most are often those who are most alive to the contrast between their ideal and their actual conditions. When it comes to the subject of history which is close to the heart of every patriot, we would seem to follow the reasonable course in avoiding

---

38   Ibid.
39   Ibid., 112.
40   Ibid., 113.
41   Ibid., 114.

Figure 2. George MacKinnon Wrong. Professor of History, University of Toronto (1883–1927). General Editor for The Champlain Society (1905–22) and President (1924–7). Photo about 1924.

tall talk and devoting closer attention than heretofore to the systematic study of our own annals.[42]

For Walker, never one for talk without action, the solution to this series of problems and challenges was the creation of The Champlain Society. Following his speech, Colby recalled later:

> The moment I sat down Sir Edmund said to me, 'Why shouldn't we have a society like that in Canada?'—to which I replied, 'No reason at all, if someone will do the work.' With his never-failing public spirit, Sir Edmund leaped into the breach and at once made it clear that he would be responsible for a serious effort. Of course his standing and his energy assured the project of adequate support.[43]

Walker then asked Professor George Wrong head of the University of Toronto History Department (Figure 2) and Dr. James Bain, chief librarian of the Toronto Public Library, to join him and Colby for a meeting in what he called "Bain's Library." That evening the broad idea for a society was sketched out—the name, according to Colby, "suggested itself by spontaneous combustion"[44]—Champlain being "the first settler and founder of the Country."[45] The following morning, Walker explained the objectives of the new society to his private secretary Eleanor Creighton, and told her "...while the others were not very sanguine as to the possibilities of starting this enterprise, he himself thought it could be done."[46] He also mentioned to her that Dr. Arthur G. Doughty, Dominion Archivist, had told him:

> ...that there were many most interesting documents and letters in the Archives in Ottawa which would be most interesting and educative could they be made available to the public, and also that there were other most important events and enterprises which should be chronicled, but that unless this was done by a private publishing society, it probably never would be done at all.[47]

The idea was to create a non-profit society dedicated to publishing rare and important books or collections of documents relating to Canada. The volumes were to be "attractive to booklovers" and would be rigorously edited by the best scholars in the field. Each volume would have a critical introduction that placed its contents in the frame of Canadian history. Membership was to be limited to 200 individuals approved

---

42 Ibid., 115.
43 Charles Colby, "Story of the founding of the Champlain Society," *The Champlain Society 42nd Annual Report* (Toronto, 1949).
44 Ibid.
45 Ibid. box 41, item 41:6. Creighton, "Memorandum," 24, and Jarvis, "Speech, Part 1," [9], recount similar stories about the founding of the Society.
46 Ibid., Creighton, "Memorandum," 24.
47 Ibid., Creighton, "Memorandum."

by Council and elected at a meeting of the Society by at least two-thirds of those present; 60 from Québec, 60 from Ontario, 40 from the Maritimes and 40 from the West. Within two weeks membership was expanded to 250 individuals and 250 libraries throughout the world. The annual membership fee was to be $10, providing an income of $5000 to cover the cost of preparing and printing two volumes per year.[48] The problem faced by Walker was how to secure enough members. As Eleanor Creighton recalled:

> So we set to work. First of all a folder was prepared, setting forth the aims and objectives of the Society. The choice of the name was obvious—Champlain having been the first white settler in Canada...Under Sir Edmund's instructions I wrote to every Manager of the Bank,[49] enclosing a folder to explain the aims of the Society, and asking him for a list of names in his locality who would, in his opinion, be interested in the aims of the Society. When these lists were sent in, circulars were sent out. Then I took the Canadian Almanac and from the list of Members of Parliament, Judges, Government officials, etc., circularized every name. In this way twenty-five hundred circulars were sent out, and the response thereto gave us exactly two hundred and fifty members—our desired quota. Next libraries were taken up, and practically every library in the world had a circular sent them. The response from libraries was somewhat slower, but eventually the two hundred and fifty were secured. The work involved in all this—very much correspondence was also included—was rather stupendous, but it got done.[50]

The response from the circulars was voluminous. Between 1905 and 1906 Walker dictated and personally signed well over five hundred pieces of correspondence.[51] A major concern of his was not to miss "prominent people" or "principal gentlemen of Canada."[52] There were repeated questions about what qualifications if any a person had to have to become a member, which led Walker at one point to write to a critic that it is:

> ...not at all necessary that they should be literary people or experienced in history; it is only necessary that they should be sufficiently interested in the undertaking [of the Society].[53]

Objections were received from some ladies that since the circular was in "masculine form" did they mean to exclude women?[54] Walker assured them that the Society was

---

48 We do not know who made the costing estimates, but they were accurate. The average cost of each of the first eight volumes (1907–1914), including editorial fees, printing and shipping was $1,902. These costs however, had risen to an average of $3307 per volume between the publication of the first (1922) and last (1936) volume of the *Works* (sixteen volumes). See Table 6.
49 Letters were sent to 35 bank managers.
50 Ibid., Creighton, "Memorandum," 25.
51 MS Coll. 50, Letter Books, Item 1 (May 1905–August 1906).
52 Ibid., 52, 56.
53 Ibid., Walker to Jack, pp. 66–67.
54 Ibid., Walker to Fitz-Randolph, p. 89, and Walker to Machar, p. 110. Both are on the "List of Original Members."

open to women; in fact seven of the first 250 members were women.⁵⁵ One writer who questioned whether the books would be a limited edition was assured it would be, "…in order that they shall thereby be certain to have a positive value in money in the future."⁵⁶ Along with the circular was an invitation to 27 prospective members to attend an inaugural meeting on May 17, 1905, in order to discuss the Aims, proposed Constitution and a slate of provisional officers for the Society. Owing to short notice and a postal delay of letters to Québec, only five attended. No changes were proposed except that membership be raised to 250 members and 250 libraries.⁵⁷ The only negative comment came from the Dominion Archivist, Arthur Doughty, who wanted to be associated with the new society, but considered that the "…interests of the country would be better served by a commission" such as the Manuscript Commission that "…would at any rate cover the same things." He also thought that the "…proposed Champlain Society would find it too difficult to get enough members."⁵⁸

On October 5, a committee was set up consisting of Edmund Walker, Professors George Wrong, Charles Colby, Adam Shortt,⁵⁹ James Bain and the archivist Arthur Doughty, to draw up a preliminary list of publications for a meeting on 30 October.⁶⁰ The committee went to work and produced the following list:

For 1906	"The Cartwright Papers, 1785–1815," by Adam Shortt.
	"The Seigniorial [sic] Tenure in Canada," in 2 vols., by W. Bennett Munro.
For 1907	"Rare Maps of Canada with a Commentary," by William Wood.
	"Bougainville Papers" (Wolfe/Montcalm period), by de Keralain.
For 1908	"Montcalm Papers," by Arthur Doughty.
	"Rebellion of 1837," by de Celles.
For 1909	"General Murray in Canada," no author proposed.
	"Louisbourg," by John S. McLennan.
For 1910	"A Social History of French Canada," by Charles Colby.
	"British Colonial Policy," by Adam Shortt.

A much longer "wish list" followed, some with potential authors but no publication dates attached to them.⁶¹ Other correspondence shows that authors were being contacted to begin work on some of these volumes, including Henry P. Biggar for a possible Champlain volume to be ready in 1908. On March 29, 1906 the Provisional

---

55 Ibid., item 66, Minute Book, 1905–1925, "List of the Original Members…" pp. 7–13 (Note: page numbers in the Minute Book are irregular and contain blanks. Numbers given here refer to consecutive pages with writing on them).
56 Ibid., item 1, Walker to Bruce, p. 75.
57 Ibid., item 66, Minute Book, 1905–1925, pp. 1–4.
58 MS Coll. 1, box 7, Doughty to Wrong, 28 April 1905.
59 Adam Shortt was professor of political science at Queen's University, Kingston, 1886–1908, and 1918–31 chairman of the Board of Historical Publications at the Public Archives.
60 MS Coll. 50, item 1, p. 105, Wrong to Colby, 5 October 1905.
61 Ibid., 129–135, Wrong to Walker, 30 October 1905.

Committee of Bain, Walker and Wrong met to settle the first membership list and set the date of the first Annual Meeting. It was decided to hold the Annual Meeting in the Board Room of the Canadian Bank of Commerce at 4 p.m. on May 10, 1906. The first membership list reads like a "Who's Who" of Canada at the time: the Prime Minister, Sir Wilfrid Laurier; leader of the Conservative party, Robert Borden; William Lyon Mackenzie King, deputy minister under Laurier and after 1921, prime minister; Sandford Fleming, surveyor and railroad engineer; the Earl Grey, Governor General; plus four Lieutenant Governors; eleven judges; twelve Members of Parliament and three Senators; twenty Canadian Bank of Commerce managers, as well as many professors, medical doctors and reverends.[62]

Three provisional officers and twenty members attended the First Annual Meeting. Walker reported that 250 members had been secured with ten more on a waiting list; in addition there were twenty subscribing libraries and a bank balance of $1,907.23.[63] George Wrong submitted a more advanced list of forthcoming publications that shows substantial changes from the one of October 30:

>"Marc Lescarbot: Histoire, vol. 1," by William L. Grant and Henry P. Biggar.
>"Denys' Description and Natural History of Northern America," by William F. Ganong.
>"Documents Relating to the Seigniorial Regime," by W. Bennet Munro.
>"The Cartwright Papers, 1778–1814," by Adam Shortt.

These four were all to be completed by the end of 1907, to make up for the two promised for 1906 and 1907![64] Also listed with no specific publication date were:

>"The Naval Records of the Conquest of Canada," by William Wood.
>"Louisbourg: From Its Foundation To Its Fall (1713–1760)," by John S. McLennan.

Last on the agenda was the election of the first slate of officers listed as follows:

President
> Dr. B.E. Walker

Vice Presidents
> Sir Louis Jetté (Lt. Governor of Québec)
> Sir D.H. McMillan (Lt. Governor of Manitoba)
> Sir Henri Joly de Lotbinière (Lt. Governor of British Columbia)[65]
> The Hon, William Clark (Lt. Governor of Ontario)
> The Hon. L.J. Tweedie (Premier of New Brunswick)

---

62 Ibid., pp. 5–13.
63 Ibid., item 66, Minute Book, 1905–1925, pp. 27–32. See Table 8.
64 Ibid., 33–35.
65 Because of his "advancing years", Lotbinière was unable to serve on Council.

Secretaries
    Prof. Charles W. Colby (McGill University)
    Prof. George Wrong (University of Toronto)[66]
Treasurer
    Dr. James Bain (Toronto Public Library)
Councilors
    Dr. A.G. Doughty (Dominion Archivist)
    Prof. Adam Shortt (Queen's University)
    Mr. H.H. Langton (Librarian, University of Toronto)
    Mr. James Coyne (Historian)
    His Honour Judge Sicotte (Montréal)[67]

The format of the books was adopted at a Council meeting on November 6, 1906. The volumes were to be:

> …the same size of pages as the new Library Edition of Ruskin's Works, and paper to be in accordance with the sample in the dummy submitted by Mssrs Ballantyne, Hanson & Co. The type to be the same as that of the Hakluyt Society's later publications…The binding is to be in red linen buckram, as per sample submitted, with gilt lettering. The volumes have the top gilt edged.[68]

The size of the Ruskin volumes is 7" by 10", slightly larger than the early Champlain Society books. The boards are red linen. The inside page has a listing of the number of copies printed and the title page contains a seal, in all much like the inside page and title page of Champlain Society publications. Needless to say, Ruskin was a favorite writer of Sir Edmund who possessed several editions.

The seal of the Society was adopted sometime before the First Annual Meeting. It was taken from the seal of the Company New France (Company of One Hundred Associates) founded in 1627. "The beautiful motto 'Thy way is in the sea' (Psalm lxxvii, 19, authorized version) is striking, when Canada's present incorporation in a great maritime empire is remembered." These lines, found on the inside page of the First Annual Report were probably written by Edmund Walker.

Conception of the Champlain Project

At the organizational meetings of The Champlain Society in 1905, the committee that had been appointed to draw up a preliminary list of potential volumes included on it a volume on *Documents Related to Champlain*. The plan was that this volume would be

---

66 George Wrong was also appointed general editor for the Society. He held the position from 1905 to 1922.
67 Ibid., 32–33.
68 Ibid., 38. The Library Edition of the *Complete Works of John Ruskin*, 39 vols (London: G. Allen, 1903–12), was edited by E.T. Cook and Alexander Wedderburn. Sir Edmund had about a dozen sets of Ruskin's writings including the 39 volume Cook and Wedderburn edition. A set of these books is in the York University Library, Special Collections, PR 5251 C6.

Figure 3. Henry Percival Biggar. Chief Archivist for Canada in Europe (1905–38). Photo published January 28, 1928, in *Saturday Night*, on the occasion of his receiving an Honorary Degree from Oxford University, England.

edited by Dr. Henry Percival Biggar,[69] (Figure 3) deputy archivist for Canada in Europe, in a similar fashion to the book of documents he was currently collecting and editing on Jacques Cartier.[70] Also on the list were volumes by Sagard, Selkirk and Durham, and a note that the Society hoped that Biggar would publish his Cartier volume with them.[71] Biggar was contacted to see if he would translate and edit the whole of Champlain's writings but declined, saying that, in view of the Otis translation for the Prince Society in 1880,[72] "I should hardly think a new translation was necessary."[73] On October 6, the proposal was repeated with an offer of a membership in The Champlain Society but Biggar turned both down. By October 30, when a much longer list of some thirty items had been drawn up, the *Documents Related to Champlain* had been changed to an edition encompassing all of Champlain's published *Works and Documents*, to be done by Biggar, even though he had not yet agreed to do the project. The completion date for the new Champlain edition was set for the Tercentenary of Québec in 1908. Colby, Bain and Shortt felt that because of the importance of Champlain to Canada, these volumes should also be sold to the public.[74] Biggar was informed of the changed proposal but declined with the words "In my humble opinion there is no necessity for a new edition of Champlain in the original. A fresh translation however should prove of interest."[75] In the hope of getting funding from the Dominion Government, the Council of the Society however, had committed themselves to a bilingual Champlain edition of "about six volumes,"[76] even though it had as yet no editor. After Biggar had agreed to help Professor William L. Grant[77] by writing the introduction to the three volumes of the 1618 edition of Lescarbot's *Histoire*,[78] he was approached again to "undertake this

---

69 Biggar (1872–1938) was perfectly bilingual and highly regarded as one of the foremost scholars on 16th and 17th century Canada, having recently published *The Early Trading Companies of New France* (Toronto: The University of Toronto Library, 1901).
70 MS Coll. 50, item 1, Letter Books, pp. 105–111.
71 Unfortunately for the Champlain Society, the Public Archives of Canada published this book. Henry P. Biggar, ed., *The Voyages of Jacques Cartier* (Ottawa: Publications of the Public Archives of Canada, no. 11, 1924).
72 Samuel de Champlain, *Voyages of Samuel De Champlain*, 3 vols, ed. Edmund Slafter, trans. Charles Pomeroy Otis (Boston: The Prince Society, 1880). [See Appendix IV].
73 MS Coll. 50, box 25, fol. 7, Biggar to Wrong, 2 September 1905.
74 Ibid., fol. 40, Wrong to Walker, 30 October 1905. Ibid., 129–135.
75 Ibid., fol. 7, Biggar to Wrong, 13 November 1905.
76 Ibid., fol. 41, Walker to Champlain Society Membership, 5 February 1906.
77 At the time William L. Grant (1872–1935) was Beit Lecturer in Colonial History at Oxford (1906–10) and from 1910 to 1917, Professor of History at Queen's University, Kingston. He was Principal of Upper Canada College from 1917 to his death.
78 MS Coll. 50, item 1, Wrong to Biggar, 2 November 1905. Marc Lescarbot, *The History of New France by Marc Lescarbot*, 3 vols., ed. William L. Grant, intro. Henry P. Biggar (Toronto: The Champlain Society, 1907–14). Volume 1, of Lescarbot was the first publication by the Society.

work [Champlain], taking your own time."⁷⁹ To Biggar however, a major commitment to Champlain was clearly too much until "the edition of Cartier is off my hands."⁸⁰

At the request of the Council of the Society, Walker and Wrong wrote a letter on November 21, 1907 to the Prime Minister, Sir Wilfrid Laurier, a founding member of the Champlain Society, requesting a grant to help defray publishing costs for a bilingual, definitive edition that would promote "growth of unity in national sentiment."⁸¹ Appended to the letter was a memo by the secretary of the Society, Joseph-Edmond Roy,⁸² a prominent French Canadian historian, containing an ambitious outline for the project as well as some editing procedures [see Appendix III]. Also included in the letter was the assurance that there would be a press run for sale to the public. What the Society requested was $1,500 a year ($5.00 per book for 300 copies), for six years ($9,000), payable when each volume appeared. The Prime Minister answered promptly explaining that the Society should make their request to a committee he was about to appoint for the tercentenary celebration of Champlain's founding of Québec, assuring them that in all likelihood some money would be available.⁸³ Fundraising was also attempted at the provincial level, with no success from any province except Québec.⁸⁴ However, even the government of Québec could only promise $300 for 60 books.⁸⁵ On March 19, 1908, an Act of Parliament established the National Battlefields Commission with $300,000 funding from the Dominion Government. The Provinces of Ontario and Québec quickly followed with another $100,000 each. The Act also called for five commissioners to be appointed by the Dominion Government, one of whom was Edmund Walker.⁸⁶ Walker was therefore both a commissioner and representative of The Champlain Society as its president. The Tercentenary was an elaborate public effort to weld the nation together and to instil a sense of patriotism in its citizens.⁸⁷ Funding for such a worthwhile project as the publication of Champlain's *Works* was regarded as a foregone conclusion and plans were laid for its realization.

---

79   Ibid., Wrong to Biggar, 9 January 1906.
80   Ibid., box 25, fol. 7, Biggar to Wrong, 26 February 1906.
81   Ibid., box 48, fol. 1, Walker to Sir Wilfrid Laurier, 21 November 1907.
82   Joseph-Edmond Roy was a notary and historian. In 1907, at the time he became involved with The Champlain Society he had just been appointed Head of the new Manuscript Division of the Public Archives in Ottawa. Yves Hébert, "Roy, Joseph-Edmond." *Dictionary of Canadian Biography: Volume 14, 1911–1920* (Toronto: University of Toronto Press, 1998).
83   Ibid., box 26, fol. 19, Laurier to Walker, 22 November 1907.
84   Ibid., fol. 35, Wrong to Walker, 11 February 1908; Wrong to Roy, 18 March 1908.
85   Ibid., Roy to Wrong, 21 April 1908.
86   Frank Carrel and Louis Feiczewicz, eds., E.T.D. Chambers, revisions, A.G. Doughty, intro., *The Quebec Tercentenary Commemorative History* (Quebec: The Daily Telegraph Printing House, 1908), 13.
87   Henry Vivian Nelles, *The Art of Nation-Building: Pageantry and Spectacle at Quebec's Tercentenary* (Toronto: University of Toronto Press, 1999).

Sometime before late October 1908, Biggar must finally have agreed, with some reservations, to be the general editor for Champlain's *Works*. On October 28, 1908, the project to publish Champlain's writings got underway with an announcement to the effect that Henry Percival Biggar had been appointed general editor.[88] A few days later Wrong outlined to Biggar that the Society wanted a bilingual edition "…like Denys[89] and Lescarbot…" and advised him to do it "…as rapidly as possible." Further, Wrong thought that Biggar could simply "…revise existing translations so to make it a practically new translation and to translate the hitherto untranslated parts" and "do many if not most of the editorial notes." In fact Wrong thought:

> I suppose you will not have to go beyond Laverdière[90] for the French text…possibly it would be well to reprint Laverdière as he stands, notes and all, translated with the text as many of them as seem now pertinent with such additions as appear necessary. Your judgment on this will, of course, be final.[91]

In all, Wrong estimated four volumes of 450 pages each, for which Biggar would receive $1000. By the end of the month Biggar replied that he was glad Champlain would be published in English and French but that the remuneration for all the editing, including revision of proofs, "…is by no means adequate" and that Adam Shortt got $1500 for editing the *Constitutional Documents*.[92] He suggested however that if Joseph-Edmond Roy could be persuaded to be fully responsible for the French text and that he, as general editor "merely revised the translation, and notes," then perhaps the offer of $1000 was adequate.[93] The French text referred to by Wrong and Biggar was the six-volume edition of Champlain's writings compiled, collated and edited by l'abbé Laverdière in 1870. It was the first collation of all the original Champlain texts and some related documents and was judged to be a triumph of Canadian scholarship. Later events show that Wrong's trust in the Laverdière edition was somewhat misplaced.

On December 7, 1908, George Wrong wrote a gentle reminder to Sir George Garneau, Chair of the Tercentenary Commission, saying that if The Champlain Society received the grant, the National Battlefields Commission would get 50 presentation copies and other copies at a "moderate price."[94] Finally, on March 29, 1909, Walker learned that

---

88   MS Coll. 50, item 66, Minute Books, 28 October 1908.
89   Nicolas Denys, *The Description and Natural History of the Coasts of North America (Acadia) by Nicholas Denys*, ed. William F. Ganong (Toronto: The Champlain Society, 1908). This was the second volume printed by the Society.
90   Samuel de Champlain, *Œuvres de Champlain publiés sous le patronage de l'Université Laval*, 2nd edition, 6 vols., ed. Charles-Honoré Laverdière (Québec: Imprimé au Séminaire par Geo.-E. Desbarats, 1870).
91   MS Coll. 50, item 3, Letterbooks, Wrong to Biggar 2 November 1908.
92   Arthur G. Doughty and Adam Shortt, eds., *Canadian Archives: documents relating to the constitutional history of Canada* (Ottawa: S.E. Dawson, 1907).
93   MS Coll. 50, box 27, fol. 7, Biggar to Wrong, 22 November 1908.
94   MS Coll. 1, box 20, Correspondence, Wrong to Garneau, 7 December 1908.

the Society had been granted $5,000 from the National Battlefields Commission and announced to the Council on April 6, and to the general membership on May 5, that the edition of Champlain's *Works* was:

> ...to be regarded as the official memorial of the Tercentenary, and is to be available for purchase by the ordinary citizens of Canada in addition to the members of the Champlain Society...this will probably mean that we shall issue a numbered edition for the members, and an edition on thinner paper for the general public...we ought to be conscious of the honour of being entrusted by the Government with the publication under our own imprint of the book that will remain for all time the memorial of the Tercentenary of the arrival of Champlain at Quebec.[95]

In a sense, Walker was right; these volumes became the most lasting "literary monument" of the Tercentenary to Champlain,[96] but the moral obligation to publish a popular edition was to burden the Society until well after the last volume of Champlain's *Works* was published.

During the winter of 1908 and spring of 1909 Biggar was in London, England, where he was able to study Champlain's original five books and Laverdière's six volume *Œuvres de Champlain* in some detail. He finally reported back to George Wrong in four letters, in which he had worked out the contents of the Champlain Society volumes in relation to the French text of the six volume Laverdière edition with some potential translator/editors (see Table 1 and Appendix IV).[97] Using the Laverdière edition as a guide, Biggar had calculated that the 350,000 word text of the *Œuvres* would mean that each of the four Champlain volumes as suggested by Wrong would be about 500 pages in length, providing the French text could be set in small type like the Champlain Society's Denys and Lescarbot volumes. If, however, the French text were the same type size as the English translation, then each volume, not counting notes, would be 930 pages long. Since speed was of the essence, he suggested using Laverdière's volumes of the *Œuvres* as a guide for the French text and the following translations of Champlain's books as guides for the English text:

Volume I   *Brief Discours*; use the 1859 Hakluyt Society translation by Alice Wilmere.[98]

Volume II   *Des Sauvages*; use the Purchas 1625 translation to be revised by William Grant.[99]

---

95   MS Col. 50, item 66, Minutes of Council, 6 April and Annual Meeting 5 May 1909.
96   Nelles, *Art of Nation Building*, 302–03.
97   Table 1 gives the concordance between the Laverdière volumes and proposed Champlain Society volumes. Appendix IV gives a detailed breakdown of the original Champlain texts.
98   Samuel de Champlain, *Narrative of a Voyage to the West Indies and Mexico in the years 1599–1602*, ed. Norton Shaw, trans. Alice Wilmere (London: The Hakluyt Society, 1859).
99   Samuel Purchas, *Hakluytus Posthumus or Purchas His Pilgrimes. Contayning a History of the World, in Sea voyages & lande Travells, by Englishmen & others*, The Fourth Part, Book VIII, Chap. VI: 1605–1619

Volume III   *Les Voyages, 1613*; use the 1880 Pomeroy Otis translation to be revised by William Ganong.[100]

Volume IV   *Voyages Et Descouvertures, 1619*; to use the 1880 translation of Pomeroy Otis to be revised by William Grant.

Volume V   *Les Voyages 1632* (Part I); to use the Annie Nettleton Bourne translation[101] to be revised by William Grant and William Ganong.

Volume VI   *Les Voyages 1632* (Part II); a new translation to be made by William Grant and William Ganong.

He further suggested that Joseph-Edmond Roy "…should be invited to edit the French text, but the general editor should have the power to alter or modify his notes." As for doing this in a hurry, he told George Wrong that: "You do not appear to realize the amount of time required in order to verify notes and clear up obscure points in work of this kind." It was a warning that became a disturbing reality as the project proceeded.[102]

After receiving Biggar's letter Wrong consulted with the Council of the Society and wrote to Biggar that they had settled on six volumes in which the French and English type had to be the same size because they had been promised Dominion Government money through the National Battlefields Commission. The budget for editing had been set at $500 per volume out of which all editing and translating fees had to be paid. Council had also decided that there would be a printing of 500 copies for the members and a "small edition" to be sold to the public. Since this would not be a "members only" limited edition like the other Champlain volumes "…we will give the members two volumes of Champlain as the equivalent of one of the strictly limited edition." Lastly, he suggested that Biggar be free to hire "ten or twelve helpers" and that he (Wrong) could help contact anyone Biggar suggested.[103]

Knowing that there would be funding for five or six volumes, Biggar was now free to begin planning in greater detail. In his next letter he suggested that the historian Professor Hugh H. Langton[104] (Figure 4) rework the *Brief Discours* from the Hakluyt Society translation and use *Des Sauvages* from the Purchas translation, checking each against the translations by Bourne and Otis. For this work he thought $100 would be adequate. If Roy was going to collate the French texts using the Laverdière edition as the base text, Biggar suggested that he "apply to the John Carter Brown Library [Providence, Rhode Island] for the loan of the MS" of the *Brief Discours* and one of the

---

      (London: William Stansby for Henrie Featherstone, 1625).
100 Samuel de Champlain, *Voyages of Samuel De Champlain*, ed. Slafter, trans. Otis.
101 Samuel de Champlain, *The Voyages and Explorations of Samuel de Champlain (1604–1616) Narrated by Himself…Together with the Voyage of 1603 Reprinted from Purchas His Pilgrimes*, ed. Edward Gaylord Bourne, trans. Annie Nettleton Bourne (New York: A.S. Barnes, 1906).
102 MS Coll. 50, box 27, fol. 7, Biggar to Wrong, 26 March 1909.
103 Ibid., item 4, Letterbooks, 1909–10, Wrong to Biggar, 7 April 1909.
104 Hugh Hornby Langton (1862–1953) was Chief Librarian, University of Toronto, from 1892 to 1923.

Figure 4. Hugh Hornby Langton. Chief Librarian, University of Toronto (1892–1923). Treasurer of The Champlain Society (1908–12; 1936–47) and President (1934–6). Photo of an oil portrait by Edmund Wyly Grier painted in 1924 when Langton retired from the University of Toronto.

original editions of *Des Sauvages*. Thinking that Laverdière had already done the basic work of collating the French texts, Biggar suggested that Roy be paid $650 for all six projected volumes. He also pointed out that there were 62 plates in the *Brief Discours*, which "will cost something" to reproduce, especially since "several are in colour."[105] For *Les Voyages 1613*, he felt that Professor William F. Ganong[106] (Figure 5) be asked to do the Acadian portion (1604 to 1607) while Professor William L. Grant was to do the St. Lawrence/Ontario section (1608 to 1613). *Les Voyages 1632* was to be split between Ganong doing the Acadian part and Grant the rest of the *Premier Partie*, while William D. LeSueur[107] (Figure 6) would deal with all of the *Seconde Partie* with the exception of the *Traitté de la Marine*, which was to go to Langton as, "…someone familiar with a yacht."[108] No allocation had yet been made for *Voyages Et Descouvertures*.

Having received the April 29 letter from Biggar, Wrong wrote to Roy, Ganong and LeSueur. Roy agreed to do the collations of the French texts, for which Wrong offered him $500, not the $650 suggested by Biggar, Ganong would do the Acadian part of *Les Voyages 1613* and LeSueur the *Seconde Partie* of *Les Voyages 1632*.[109] In his reply to Wrong, Biggar suggested that Ganong be paid $65 for his part of the 1613 text and agreed that a remuneration of $500 to Roy "should be sufficient." A snag however had developed with the *Brief Discours*, because the John Carter Brown Library would not permit borrowing the manuscript. Instead, Biggar suggested, Roy could go to Providence, collate the manuscript, and while there ask to see the original edition of *Des Sauvages*. For the *Traitté de la Marine* he suggested that Dr. Samuel Dawson[110] might be asked, "if he would not think it too great a nuisance."[111] The translation and editing of the remainder of the 1613 Voyage and the *Voyages Et Descouvertures*, Biggar hoped, would be done by Grant, "…but the poor fellow is overwhelmed with other work at present so it will be better to say nothing to him for the present." He also learned that Roy would not be able to go to Providence and now hoped the University of Toronto

---

105 Here Biggar was mistaken. All 62 plates are in colour.
106 William Francis Ganong (1864 –1941) was Professor of Botany, Smith College, Northampton, Massachusetts. He was a well-respected historian of Acadia, a Mi'kmaq linguist and had extensive experience with Champlain's writings.
107 William Dawson Le Sueur (1840–1917) was a Civil Servant in the Post Office, Ottawa. He was a well-known author and critic who served as president of the Royal Society of Canada from 1912–13. Clifford G. Holland, "LeSueur, William Dawson," *Dictionary of Canadian Biography: Volume 14, 1911–1920* (Toronto: University of Toronto Press, 1998)
108 MS Col. 50, box 27, fol. 7. Biggar to Wrong, 29 April 1909.
109 Ibid., box 27, fol. 17, Wrong to Roy, 12 May 1905; Ganong to Wrong, 17 May 1909; Biggar to Wrong, 1 June 1909; Roy to Wrong, 5 June 1909.
110 Dr. Samuel Edward Dawson (1833–1916) had published on John Cabot and Champlain's maps. He was a member of the Royal Society of Canada who had helped Biggar with *The Precursors of Jacques Cartier, 1497–1534* (Ottawa, 1911). In 1890, he had written an eight page privately printed epic poem, *Champlain*, for the "Montreal Pen and Pencil Club."
111 MS Col. 50, box 27, fol. 7, Biggar to Wrong, 1 June 1909.

Figure 5. William Francis Ganong. Naturalist, historian of matters pertaining to Acadia, the Mi'kmaq and cartography. Professor of Botany, Smith College, Northampton, Massachusetts, 1893–1924. Photo taken in 1913, at the time he was working on the Champlain volumes.

Figure 6. William Dawson LeSueur. Man of letters, civil servant, historian, social critic. Photo about 1912 on his election as President of the Royal Society of Canada.

Library could secure the original manuscript of *Brief Discours* and *Des Sauvages* from the John Carter Brown Library.[112]

To this point nothing much had been said about editing procedures except that as general editor, Biggar was to have final say in everything pertaining to the French and English texts and accompanying notes. In reacting to a review of his editorial work on *The Description and Natural History* by Nicholas Denys for The Champlain Society, Ganong had gone on record that:

> ...the only logical and honest way [to reproduce a text] seems to me to reproduce letter for letter, including the errors, peculiarities of printing and all, and I propose to continue the same method in the future...".[113]

A year later he pursued the subject again, this time with Walker, who wrote Wrong that he hoped that Ganong's ideas for a definitive edition would be followed and not Biggar's, who evidently wanted a French text that avoided spelling errors and archaic usages.[114] This matter was to surface at frequent intervals through the project.

By May 1910 a budget had been worked out on the basis of a six-volume set. The cost per volume was estimated at $4.00, with a six-volume set costing $24.00. Since the membership of The Champlain Society was about 400 and 100 sets were to go the National Battlefields Commission, the total cost of Champlain's *Works* was estimated at $12,000. The decision was then made to use the $5000.00 grant from the National Battlefields Commission to subsidize the member's edition by charging each member only $15.00 per set. This would bring in $7,500.00, which, with the subsidy, would yield a profit of $500 for the Society. The "Popular Edition" was to be printed after the Member's Edition had been published. No cost estimates were made, but 900 sets were to be printed on "commercial style paper" and sold for $15.00 per set ($2.50 per volume), bringing in $13,500.00.[115]

During 1910, most of the arrangements regarding the project had been put in place. The prospect for a rapid start and a soon to be completed first volume seemed assured. Ganong was about to begin the translation of *Les Voyages, 1613*, Langton thought he might have *Brief Discours* and *Des Sauvages* done by the end of the summer and Roy was rumoured to have found only "one or two slips in Laverdière's text."[116] The only outstanding item was the reproduction of the plates for the *Brief Discours* since no arrangements had yet been made with the John Carter Brown Library.[117] Biggar also

---

112 Ibid., Biggar to Wrong, 22 June 1909.
113 Ibid., box 27, fol. 17, Ganong to Wrong, 8 April 1909.
114 Ibid., box 28b, fol. 33, Walker to Wrong, 19 October 1910.
115 Ibid., item 66, Minute Books, p. 106. The first grant of $2,500 by the Battlefields Commission was made on May 2, 1911.
116 Ibid., box 28a, fol. 3, Biggar to Wrong, 5 May 1910.
117 Ibid., box 28b, fol. 33, Doughty to Wrong, 9 November 1910.

raised the question whether the 62 plates that went with the manuscript text could be done in colour.[118] When Wrong consulted Walker on the subject his response was that:

> All the Champlain illustrations apart from the maps are grotesque and uninteresting, but I presume they should be copied, colours and all, unless it is too expensive to do so.[119]

Near the end of 1910 came the first substantive sign that editing and translating was underway when Le Sueur submitted his translation of the text for Volume V to the Society. A couple of weeks later Walker sent a letter to Wrong that Le Sueur be paid his fee of $100.[120]

It was unfortunate that it took four years before Champlain's *Works* were at last underway. Funding had to be established; Biggar had to be persuaded to become general editor; a francophone editor had to be found and three of the main editor/translators, Biggar, Grant and Ganong were busy with other volumes. To place the Champlain edition in perspective, by 1910, when Champlain's *Works* finally began, the Society had already published five volumes (Table 2 a).[121] Besides these volumes fifteen more had been accepted and were in preparation. Of the published volumes, Lescarbot, Denys and Le Clercq were originally in French and were produced as fully edited translations with the original French text in smaller type at the end of each volume. The French documents in the Munro volume were not translated, but the Louisbourg and La Vérendrye volumes were to be similar in style to Lescarbot, Denys and Le Clercq. Rapid progress with Champlain's *Works* was expected because it was thought that these volumes would resemble the complexity of those already published or underway. Moreover, it was thought that in view of the collated French text by Laverdière, progress might actually be faster. The problem as it turned out was that familiarity with Lescarbot, Denys, Le Clercq and La Vérendrye was no safe guide to Champlain's writings and unfortunately no one in the Society had thought of conducting a study into the complexity of Champlain's original texts, maps, illustrations and the existence of further documents.

It was unfortunate for the speedy editing of the first volume of Champlain's *Works* that Biggar was also involved with the Lescarbot volumes and Ganong with *Denys* and *Le Clercq* (Table 2 a). Therefore nothing could be done to speed them up. Everything that related to a project, from the initial proposal involving time estimates and content,

---

118   Ibid., box 28a, fol. 40, Wrong to Walker, 11 November 1910.
119   Ibid., fol. 33, Walker to Wrong, 14 November 1910.
120   Ibid., item 6, Letter Books, August 1910 to November 1911, Walker to Wrong, 22 December 1910.
121   MS Coll. 50, item 66, Minute Book, 1905–1926. This list was collated from dated entries written between 1905 and 1911 in the Minute Book. Provisional titles, potential editors and dates are as in the hand written entries.

to the typing of the final manuscript was the responsibility of the editor(s). The Society took the responsibility for a copy edit by the general editor, all dealings with the press and the distribution of the book. If the Society was unhappy about the progress of a particular volume there was little they could do about it, short of cancellation. Lack of an adequate financial reward for editing a volume made a contract meaningless; therefore there were no contracts in a modern sense, only an agreement between colleagues. In a very real sense, for many editors the production of a book for the Society was done out of interest if time permitted, and some editors could not or would not be hurried.

George Wrong and Edmund Walker clearly presided over an ambitious publications program that had to undergo a number of adjustments. The first membership invoice had been sent out in 1905 but the first two publications did not appear until 1907 and 1908 (see Table 2 a, and 4).[122] By this time it was clear that the process of getting books into print was going to be much slower than first anticipated. Instead of two volumes per year for a fee of $10 it appeared that, for a while at least, the Society was going to average one book per year. Thinking that the slow progress getting the books into print would be temporary, an adjustment in billing the membership was made. Instead of a yearly fee an invoice was sent "when called for," that is, when two books had been published or were about to be published. The second invoice for publications three and four was sent in 1908 and the members got one book in 1909 and the second one in 1910 (see Table 4). In 1914, the sixth invoice entitled them to publication eleven printed that year and number twelve which was not printed until 1917. It was frustrating to the executive and the Council that of the 27 volumes launched before 1914 only nine were completed, another three paid for by the membership but not yet published and four cancelled for various reasons (see Tables 2 a, 2 b, and 4). The membership of course was confused. Initially, dues paid by members that were not "called for" through an invoice, were returned; later the members were credited toward a future volume. From 1917 to 1931 the members received only one publication for their $10 fee whenever a volume appeared in print. Reasons given for the slow output of publications were everything from marauding German submarines to the escalating price of paper. From 1932 to 1951 however, the Society reverted to two volumes per year for a fee of $10. From 1938 to 1949 the Hudson's Bay Series assured the increased output of publications.[123] In 1948 fees were raised to $15 per year and in 1952, with the publication of Robinson and Conacher's second volume of Du Creux's *History of Canada or New France*, the Society permanently moved to one publication per year for a membership fee of $15.

---

122 Ibid., box 18, fol. 9, "Explanation of fees paid," no date.
123 Sir Campbell Stewart, Governor of the H.B.Co., terminated the agreement between the Hudson's Bay Record Society and the Champlain Society on 30 December 1948. Basically the Company wanted an open membership and keep fees at $10 per year. Ibid., item 67, written minutes from 1947 to the end of 1948. The last Hudson's Bay volume *Isham's Observation and Notes, 1743–49* was a gift by the Company to the Champlain Society.

EDITING *THE WORKS OF SAMUEL DE CHAMPLAIN*, 1905–1939

> The only logical and honest way [to reproduce the text] seems to me to reproduce letter for letter, including the errors, peculiarities of printing and all, and I propose to continue the same method in the future. *William F. Ganong, April 1909.*

> The method we have followed is that adopted by the editors of the Société de l'Histoire de France…I have no intention [therefore] of putting commas in wrong places nor of writing *il y à* because the original happens to have these. *Henry P. Biggar, August 1928.*

Editing the First Volume

The editorial procedures that were worked out, or not worked out, reveal a naiveté that can only be excused because the Society was in its infancy. Henry Biggar had been appointed general editor of the project and as such had been given control over all editorial work. Unfortunately, he was almost never in Canada to work at first hand with his translator-editors. All correspondence was by trans-oceanic mail. A local coordinator for the project was therefore necessary and that role fell to Professor George Wrong, secretary and general editor for the Society, and a very busy man as head of Modern History at the University of Toronto. By 1910, two scholars had been appointed to help Biggar who were fluent in modern French and had strengths in other fields, sufficient it was assumed, to undertake the translation as well as the scholarly editing of the sections for which they were responsible. For the first volume, these were Hugh Langton and William Ganong, with the French text to be collated by Joseph-Edmond Roy, whose qualifications, as head of the Manuscript Division of the Public Archives of Canada were impeccable.

The faith the Society and its editors had in the Laverdiére edition is in retrospect difficult to understand until it is placed in the context of the times during which the Champlain project was being conceived. At that time the Laverdiére edition had been the largest undertaking in Canadian scholarly publishing and upon its completion in 1870, had met with universal critical acclaim. The initiators of the Champlain project were well aware of that reputation. Just as the Society's project was being finalized, l'abbé Auguste Gosselin, a highly respected French Canadian historian, added to that reputation with a lyrical retrospect of Laverdiére's work published in the Memoirs of the

Royal Society of Canada. His claim was that Laverdière's *Œuvres De Champlain* was the "true monument" to Champlain, not the magnificent statue raised to the *"foundateur de Québec"* at Québec in 1898.[1] The Champlain Society Council and its editors, many of whom were members of the Royal Society, were well aware of Gosselin's paper, thus reinforcing the opinion they already had of Laverdiére's work.[2]

Getting started was no problem, or so it seemed. Based on the assumption that the 1870 edition, *Œuvres De Champlain,* edited by the Abbé Laverdière, was a nearly perfectly collated and edited French text, Biggar, Wrong and the Council of the Society thought that a cursory look at the original texts would disclose few problems and might not even be necessary. In fact, it would save time and money to simply reprint the French text by Laverdière with the English translation. Therefore the operating procedure became straightforward. A set of the 6-volume Laverdiére text was purchased, cut up, and each translator/editor was given the task of translating and editing his section(s). The minor corrections that Roy might find in Laverdière's collated text could simply be penciled in before it went to the printer.

By December 1910, complaints reached George Wrong as coordinator of the publications, that Champlain was "a disorderly writer…formless of style…[and that]… a phrase by phrase translation is utterly impossible."[3] Others, particularly Ganong, complained that there should be an editorial policy regarding spelling and footnotes. He wanted French and English text and notes on the same page, not at the end of the book as had been done with Lescarbot, Denys and Le Clercq and suggested that the French text be rendered as a photo facsimile.[4] He also wanted to keep the original spellings of all names; not to modernize them as Biggar wanted.[5] Biggar eventually drew up some guidelines following Ganong's suggestions for the notes, but insisted on modern spellings for all names. By this time Biggar had concurred that translating Champlain posed difficulties: "I never before in my life dealt with so disorderly a writer as Champlain."[6] In his assessment of Champlain's writing abilities, Biggar found support from William Grant, who had some experience with Champlain's writings, that in Champlain we have: "The jog-trot pedestrian style, for the most part as simple and undistinguished as that of an Ontario schoolboy."[7] Grant added the suggestion that to speed up the translation and give "guidance" to the translators, the Champlain

---

1   Auguste Gosselin, "Le vrai monument de Champlain: ses Œuvres éditées par Laverdière," *Mémoires de la Société royale du Canada,* Troisième série (1908–1909) volume II, Section I, 3–23.
2   Samuel de Champlain, *The Works of Samuel de Champlain,* vol. 1, ed., Henry P. Biggar (Toronto: The Champlain Society, 1922), xvi.
3   MS Col. 50, box 48, fol. 2, Le Sueur to Wrong, 16 December 1910.
4   Ibid., Ganong to Wrong, 4 November 1911.
5   Ibid., Ganong to Wrong, 8 March 1912.
6   Ibid., Biggar to Wrong, 9 November 1911.
7   Ibid., fol. 3, Grant to Biggar, 27 September 1913.

Society seek permission from the publisher, Charles Scribner's Sons, to use Grant's recent revision of the Prince Society's 1880 edition of Champlain's *Voyages*.[8] Permission was sought and granted early the next year.[9] In fairness to Champlain, it must be said that none of the translators were specialists in sixteenth and early seventeenth century French, except Professor J. Home Cameron of the University of Toronto French Department, who was not appointed to the project until early 1918.

During 1910 it became obvious that Grant was lagging behind in getting the Lescarbot volumes finished. Pestered by continuous reminders from the executive, especially Wrong, he simply replied he had more urgent things to do. This led to severe criticism by Walker about Grant's "unspeakable" behaviour. Somehow Grant heard about Walker's opinion of him and responded that the only "unspeakable thing" was the amount of work he had put into the Lescarbot volumes. This response led Walker to suggest that the remainder of Lescarbot be turned over to Ganong, remarking again about the "intolerable lack of appreciation of his [Grant's] obligations to the Society."[10]

Early in the New Year, Ganong was pulled out of the Champlain project to do the "local notes" for the third Lescarbot volume. By this time Ganong had done a "rough translation" of his section for the first Champlain volume, which he hoped to send Biggar by "next winter" (i.e. 1911 to 1912). All he had to finish were the notes and the "little maps"[11] (Figures 7 and 8). Biggar had hoped to get Ganong's work by early June,[12] because, except for the French text, he had already received Langton's translations for *Des Sauvages* and the *Brief Discours*.[13] In spite of any news on Roy's progress with the French text, the members of the Society were given to understand that "Biggar was making rapid progress," although it was not yet possible to give publication dates due to the complications raised by the 62 plates for the *Brief Discours*.[14] It is probable that Biggar's April letter to Wrong (Appendix V) in time for the May Annual Meeting was the source of this optimism. He had not written for several months and had evidently reviewed the entire project in some detail. Judging from this letter it seems that Biggar must have requested from George Parker Winship, Head Librarian at the John Carter

---

8   Samuel de Champlain, *Voyages of Samuel De Champlain, 1604–1618*, ed., William L. Grant (New York: Charles Scribner's Sons, 1907). The original translation was made by Dr. Charles Pomeroy Otis for the Prince Society (1880). Grant re-worked the Otis translation of the 1613 and 1619 *Voyages*, with additional notes. He did not include *Des Sauvages*, which was included in the Prince Society edition.
9   MS Col. 50, box 48, fol. 4, Langton to Biggar, 16 January 1914.
10 Ibid., box 28b, fol. 33, Walker to Wrong, 14 November 1910.
11 Ibid., fol. 14, Ganong to Biggar, 3 May 1911. In July Ganong wrote that he was traveling to see the localities Champlain had mapped. Ibid., fol. 14, Ganong to Wrong, 5 July 1911.
12 Ibid., Ganong to Wrong, 3 May 1911.
13 Ibid., Biggar to Wrong, 15 April 1911 (see appendix V). Langton was paid $100 for his work on 1 May 1911. Ibid., item 15, General Ledger 1906–1962.
14 Ibid., item 66, Minute Book (1905–1925), Annual Meeting, 3 May 1911.

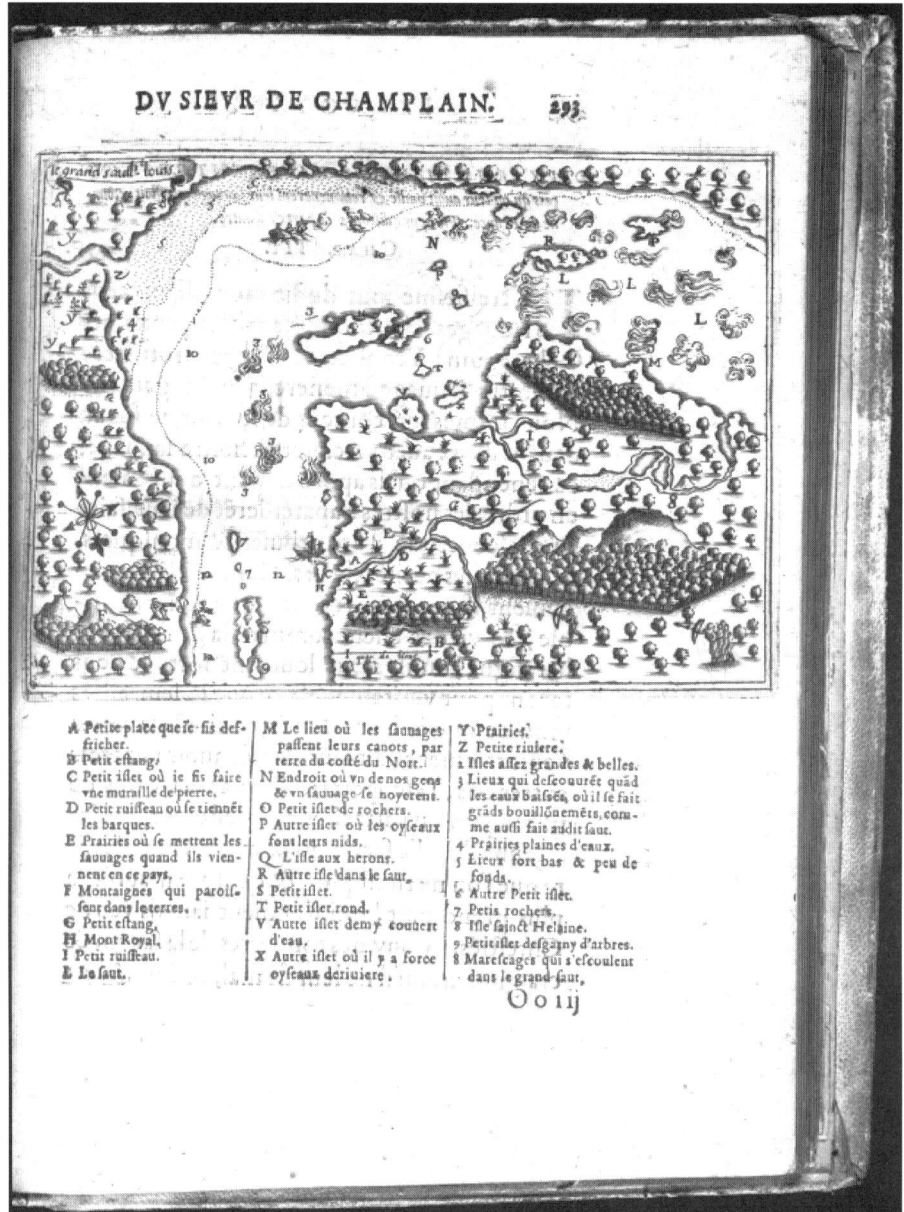

Figure 7. Champlain's map *le grand sault* st *louis* covering Montreal Island and the Lachine Rapids. In order to interpret Champlain's maps, William Ganong drew sketch maps of the same areas, often after having visited them. These sketches were inserted adjacent to Champlain's maps in *The Works*. Compare Figures 7 and 8.

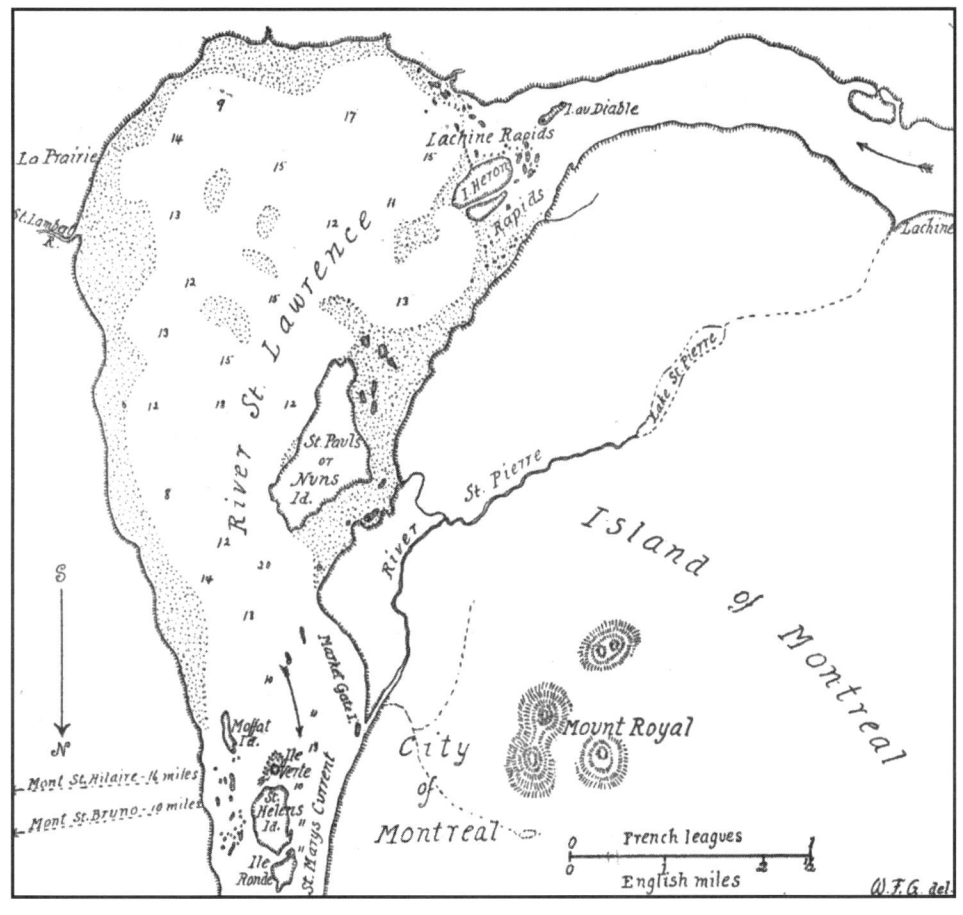

Figure 8. William Ganong's sketch map accompanying Champlain's *le grand sautl ^st louis*, covering the same area as Figure 7.

Brown Library,[15] that he undertake the collation of the French texts of *Brief Discours* and *Des Sauvages*. As the letter shows, Biggar was still under the mistaken impression that only four of the 62 plates of the *Brief Discours* "are in colour and should be reproduced in colour."[16]

The plates for *Brief Discours* were a concern and needed Walker's advice. Upon reviewing the rather poorly redrawn versions in Laverdière's *Œuvres*, Walker's suggestion was to reduce the illustrations to the page size of the Society's books, but to reproduce the maps for the volume full size. Being an expert on illustrations of the period, he considered the plates to have:

> ...very little value, are badly drawn, unreliable, I am sure, to facts, and rather below the average of illustrations accompanying old books on travel."[17]

Sensing that the illustrations might be cut, Biggar argued otherwise and urged that Winship be contacted to see if the entire West Indian Voyage (*Brief Discours*) could be done in facsimile. To drive his point home Biggar observed that: "If this edition is not to be superior in every way to Laverdière, why reprint the French text at all?"[18] Walker had the final say, explaining that the Society was bound by the grant from the National Battlefields Commission to do both texts the same size, French above and English below, and that Wrong was to travel to Boston to meet with Winship, see the West Indian material and explore the possibility of a facsimile edition.[19]

Early in May 1912, Biggar sent his usual up-date to Wrong for the May Annual Meeting. Langton had finished translating the *Brief Discours* and *Des Sauvages*. Ganong was about to send him the translation for his section of *Les Voyages, 1613*, and was working on the maps, but nothing had been heard from Roy regarding the collation of the French text causing Biggar to remark, "I think it would be more satisfactory to select a new French editor."[20] At the Annual Meeting however, the tardiness of Roy was not mentioned and the delay in the Champlain volume was blamed on the effort to finish Lescarbot III involving Grant, Ganong and Biggar. It was now hoped that the end of 1912 would see the finished first Champlain volume.[21] Biggar's irritation with Roy grew to the point where he wrote Wrong that: "Roy is impossible. He has not written

---

15 George Parker Winship was active as Chief Librarian of the John Carter Brown Library from 1895 to 1915.
16 Ibid., box 28a, fol. 3, Biggar to Wrong, 15 April 1911 [appendix V].
17 Ibid., item 6, Letter Books, August 1910–November 1911. Walker to Wrong, 27 October 1911.
18 Ibid., box 28b, fol.3, Biggar to Wrong, 18 November 1911; fol. 39, Wrong to Walker, 29 November 1911.
19 Ibid., item 7, Letter Books, November 1911–January 1913. Walker to Wrong, 1 December 1911; Walker to Biggar, 6 December 1911.
20 Ibid., box 28b, fol. 3, Biggar to Wrong, 8 May 1912.
21 Ibid., item 66, Minute Book (1905–1925), Annual Meeting, 29 May 1912.

for over two years although I have sent letter after letter."²² In fact Roy had passed away on 8 May 1913, before Biggar could get an answer from him whether he had done any work on the French texts.

Late in the summer of 1913, Langton and Ganong began to express some discomfort with the Laverdière collation. To put his translator-editors at ease and having received nothing from Roy, Biggar wrote on 24 October to Ernest Myrand,²³ chief librarian at the Québec Legislature and secretary of the Committee on History and Archaeology for the National Battlefields Commission, with a proposal to check Laverdière's texts because they seemed to be "inexact in a few places."²⁴ Myrand, who was thoroughly familiar with Champlain's writings and had access to the original texts, sent back an abruptly worded cable to Walker asking if he was to correct the French from page proofs or compare Laverdière to the original texts.²⁵ Walker returned a cable asking Myrand to begin comparing the Laverdière collation to the originals, observing to Biggar that Myrand seemed to be an "irritable type of gentleman. I am not quite sure that he reads English readily." Immediately after sending his cable to Walker, Myrand sent an "Agreement" he had drafted to George Wrong in which he stated that he would be the proofreader and sub-editor of the French texts by inserting occasional notes. Even though he insisted Laverdière's collation of the French texts was perfect, he would test it by examining 25 pages of each text against each of the original Champlain editions and would proofread all of the *Brief Discours* against a photo facsimile he hoped would be sent to him from the John Carter Brown Library. For this Myrand wanted $400.²⁶ It became evident to Walker and Wrong that Myrand did not understand what he was being asked to do. In a further letter to Myrand, Walker tried to clear up the misunderstanding but concluded privately to Wrong that: "…we have made another unfortunate selection [in a French editor]."²⁷ Before the end of December the Champlain Society had sent Myrand Laverdière's *Des Sauvages* and the *Brief Discours* both of which had already been translated and edited by Langton. Shortly after receiving the packet of texts Myrand threatened to return them because his "Agreement" had not yet been signed and he wanted more money in view of the extra work.²⁸ A few weeks later, a letter from Biggar arrived for Myrand asking him to compare the packet of Laverdière texts to Champlain's originals as well as the originals to Langton's edited Champlain Society

---

22 Ibid., box 28b fol. 3, Biggar to Wrong, 1 August 1912.
23 It was Walker who mentioned Myrand to Biggar. Ibid. item 8, Letter Books January to December 1913, Walker to Biggar, 23 September 1913. It is probable that Walker became acquainted with Myrand through the meetings of the National Battlefields Commission.
24 MS Col. 50, box 28b, fol. 3, Biggar to Myrand, 24 October 1913.
25 Ibid., item 8, Walker to Biggar, 29 October 1913. Myrand's cable was sent October 27.
26 Ibid., box 28b, fol. 4. Myrand probably sent this "Agreement" to Wrong on 28 October 1913. Letter is missing.
27 Ibid., item 8, Walker to Myrand, 19 November, and Walker to Wrong, 19 November 1913.
28 Ibid., box 28b, fol. 3. Myrand to Champlain Society, 31 December 1913.

texts to see for himself that Laverdière's work was "not perfect."[29] Myrand returned with a blistering letter to a startled Sir Edmund Walker.[30] His immediate objection was that it was an insult to Laverdière and Québec scholarship to suggest that there might be "imperfections" in the text:

> Laverdière studied them [the texts], compared them, discussed them, annotated them, in short he passed the fifteen best years of his life before publishing Champlain."[31]

From this letter it is apparent that Myrand was misled or misunderstood what he was being asked to do. From the packet of texts he had received, he thought that Biggar was requesting him to check every word in Laverdière's edition against all the texts of all the editions in the library; 1,920,000 words by Myrand's calculation, and then read all the proofs, which brought his estimated word count to 2,380,000, concluding that he was not prepared to make "an astonishing gift" of so much work to the Society for a mere $400. On January 31, Myrand quit and was sent his unsigned "Agreement" by return mail. Why the various bilingual editors of the Society did not correspond with Myrand in French is unfathomable.

Knowing that a French editor was needed, Arthur Doughty suggested "Mlle Mance or Fauteux."[32] In the meantime Langton had gone to Québec to check on the original *Des Sauvages* Laverdière was supposed to have used, only to discover that Canada did not have an original printing, and that in fact Laverdiére had "relied for two of the voyages upon copies [hand written transcriptions] of the originals made by friends in Paris."[33] In a following letter he suggested to Biggar that Professor J. Home Cameron, a specialist in the French of Champlain's period at the University of Toronto, be contacted to collate the French texts[34] (Figure 9). Fearing criticism to using English Canadian editors to collate French texts, Biggar wanted a French editor, and suggested Professor Paul Cultru of the Sorbonne.[35] Early in May, Cultru agreed to collate and edit

---

29 Ibid., fol. 4. Biggar to Myrand, 15 January 1914.
30 George V knighted Edmund Walker in 1910.
31 MS Col. 50, box 28b, fol. 4, Myrand to Walker, 28 January 1914.
32 Ibid., fol. 5, Doughty to Walker, 3 February, 1914. Fauteux was probably Aegidius Fauteux, librarian and historian at the Bibliothèque Saint Sulpice. Who Mlle Mance was is not known.
33 Ibid., fol. 5, Langton to Walker, 3 February 1914. The "two voyages were *Des Sauvages* and the *Brief Discours*. This news should not have come as a surprise since Laverdière credits l'abbé Hospice-Anthelme Verreau with copying the texts for him, *Œuvres de Champlain*, vol. I, Preface: ii; II: iii.
34 Ibid., Langton to Biggar, 11 February 1914. Professor John Home Cameron (c. 1865–1944) was Head of the French Department at University College, Toronto, from 1916–1927. He preferred to be called J. Home Cameron.
35 Ibid., Biggar to Langton, 27 February 1914, and fol. 6, Langton to Walker, 9 March 1914. Biggar also knew that Cultru would have access to a complete set of original Champlain editions in Paris. He agreed that Cameron be contacted if Cultru could not do it.

Figure 9. John Home Cameron. Professor of French, University of Toronto (1891–1927). Photo about 1925, from: John Squair, *The Autobiography of a French Teacher* (Toronto: U. of T. Press 1928): 184.

Des Sauvages, with the understanding that if his work proved to be necessary and was satisfactory, he would get to do the other volumes.[36]

By this time Walker was becoming increasingly irritated at the slow progress of Volume I. On May 19, he wrote to George Wrong: "I can no longer meet my friends in Quebec without repeating apologies for our delay already made too often."[37] To speed up translation of the later volumes, Biggar requested that Langton and Ganong get permission from the American publisher A.S.Barnes to use the translation of Champlain's books by Gaylord Bourne and Annie Nettleton Bourne.[38] Through a request by Langton, permission was granted a few weeks later.[39] Early in September Langton had finished his translation of Volume III, and LeSueur his part of Volume VI, joining Langton and Ganong's earlier translation of the books in Volume I.[40] This good news led Sir Edmund to enquire when the first volume would appear in print.[41] A month later however, Cultru informed them that he had to stop collating *Des Sauvages* because of the recent outbreak of war, and in November he returned the text to Biggar with "numerous corrections."[42] The warning by Cultru, that the Laverdière text needed correcting was unfortunately shelved for the time being as Biggar began looking for a press and editing Langton and Ganong's work for the first volume. His suggestion that the publisher Ballantyne in London, England, be approached, was approved by Sir Edmund with little thought that the war might disrupt their publishing schedule.[43]

Biggar's editing of Langton's translation seemed to go fairly smoothly, but not so the work of Ganong. In a letter to Walker, Biggar complained that Ganong was not using Grant's revision of Otis but simply copied Otis' "poor translation" and added "interminable footnotes," with the result that the editing took double the time it should.[44] His frustrations were put more forcefully in a letter to Langton, "Ganong's translation is driving me to drink. He has no more idea of English than the man in the moon, though he seems to have ferreted out the meaning of the French remarkably well."[45] As it turned out, Ganong had done his own translation of *Les Voyages, 1613*, and

---

36 Ibid., fol. 6, Biggar to Langton, 12 May 1914.
37 Ibid., Walker to Wrong, 19 May 1914.
38 Ibid., Biggar to Langton, 21 June 1914. Champlain, *The Voyages and explorations of Samuel de Champlain (1604–1616)*, ed. Bourne, trans. Nettleton Bourne.
39 Ibid., Langton to A.S. Barnes & Co., 4 July 1914. Letter of permission from Barnes on July 10.
40 Ibid., fol. 7, Biggar to Creighton, 6 September 1914
41 Ibid., Walker to Biggar, 18 September 1914.
42 Ibid., Biggar to Creighton, 3 October 1914, and fol. 8, Biggar to Walker, 5 November 1914. Eleanor Creighton was Walker's private secretary and secretary of the Society until late October 1914.
43 Ibid., fol. 8, Biggar to Walker, 5 November 1914. Ibid., Walker to Biggar, 26 November 1914. In the letter of 26 November, Walker inquired what the "difficulties with the text" were, but did not get an answer.
44 Ibid., Biggar to Walker, 5 November 1914.
45 Ibid., fol. 9, Biggar to Langton, 11 January 1915.

only used Otis as a check.[46] By early February 1915, the *Brief Discours* and *Des Sauvages* were ready for the printer although Biggar still had worries about "some words" in the translation.[47] The Ballantyne Press received the manuscript on April 7, and returned the first 80 pages of proofs to Walker on July 27, with another 176 pages on August 20.[48] By 1 September 1915, all of Volume I had been proofread by Walker and Langton and was about to go to Ganong.[49] What is astonishing in this process is that Walker, an extremely busy man as president of the Canadian Bank of Commerce, took the time to proofread the galleys. This was not a passive process; he made numerous comments, as well as suggested the necessity of giving the scientific nomenclature for birds, animals and plants. Also astonishing is that the galleys travelled safely back and forth across the ocean during wartime.

When Ganong received the page proofs of his work he decided at first to take his complaints to Walker rather than Biggar and Langton. He asserted that his translation was "*de novo*," with "little hints" from Otis. Further, he stated that he had sent Biggar an introductory "critical and descriptive sketch" for *Les Voyages, 1613*, including an essay on Champlain's method of making maps. None of these were among the page proofs.[50] Walker in turn reminded Ganong that Biggar was responsible for the Introduction with material supplied by the sub-editors like him.[51] Ganong was not the only one who received criticism. Biggar considered Langton's translation of *Des Sauvages* "too free and corrected it…to make it literate almost to baldness," leading Wrong to the opinion that through these changes, Biggar had made "Champlain a better writer [in English] than he was in French."[52] Ganong now took his problems directly to Biggar, objecting that Biggar was making a literary work out of the original and pointed out that he was wrong when he changed the meaning of some words in his translation; for example the word *gibier*, which Ganong had translated as "waterfowl" and Biggar had changed to "game." Ganong's point was that Champlain consistently used *gibier* when he was describing waterfowl, and insisted that this is what the word meant in Champlain's time.[53] Not content, Ganong now returned to Walker by sending him his corrections of the page proofs "on account of the way he [Biggar] had treated my

---

46   Ibid., fol. 10, Ganong to Walker, 10 September 1915.
47   Ibid., fol. 9, Biggar to Langton, 5 February 1915.
48   Ibid., Walker to Biggar, 27 July, 13 August, 20 August 1915.
49   Ibid., fol. 10, Langton to Walker, 1 September 1915.
50   Ibid., fol. 10, Ganong to Walker, 10 September 1915.
51   Ibid., Walker to Ganong, 17 September, and Wrong to Walker, 8 October 1915.
52   Ibid., Langton to Ganong, 20 September 1915. In 1911, Ganong had written to Wrong that Biggar should be making a more scholarly edition that "will come as near as possible to saying the last word on the subject," rather than an edition for general use. Ibid., box 28a fol. 14, Ganong to Wrong, 11 October 1911.
53   Ibid., Ganong to Biggar, 24 September 1915. Ganong was the only naturalist among the editors and had published a paper bearing on the subject. William F. Ganong, "The Identity of the Animals and Plants

manuscript."[54] Evidently Walker consulted with Langton, who wrote him that since Biggar is the general editor, he must be supported in the standards he chose to apply.[55] Walker of course agreed, trying at the same time to be conciliatory. In his letter to Biggar he said that he saw himself as "trying to keep the various threads together...and not as exercising editorial supervision." He also added, with a nod to Ganong, that all agreed Champlain "often says what he does not really mean," and that in translating him one should give the meaning and in a footnote, the textual difficulties. Finally, he noted that Ganong's introduction on Champlain's mapping was an "excellent piece of work."[56] The complaints from Ganong and sometimes Langton about Biggar's editing kept on repeating themselves to the end of the project. In a later letter to Biggar, Walker stressed that Biggar's role was to see that there is uniformity through the volumes; to shorten notes without taking out information unless it was trivial; to be indulgent with his sub-editors rather than severe and to avoid controversy and criticism with what they had written.[57]

Up to this point no definitive editorial procedures had been formulated for the contributors. Such as there were had evolved piecemeal as the project proceeded. Late in 1915, the experiences gained from the eleven Champlain Society volumes published to that date were brought together with the "in house rules" used by Ballantyne Press into a guide for potential editors.[58] The complexity of the Champlain project however, was such that continuous arguments between the general editor and sub-editors over editorial detail were inevitable, and would dog the project to its completion.

Amid these editorial squabbles came a good piece of news. From his contacts, Ganong had heard that the Library of Congress in Washington had just acquired Champlain's manuscript map of 1607, and that he had asked them for a photo.[59] After receiving a couple of poor photostats early in 1916, Ganong finally got his long-awaited glossy photo just before Christmas.[60] The arrival of this large and important map, along with the anticipated illustrations by Champlain in the *Brief Discours* and other maps to follow, prompted a re-examination of the format the *Works* were to take. Biggar

---

mentioned by the early Voyagers to Eastern Canada and Newfoundland," *Transactions of the Royal Society of Canada*, Section II (1909): 197–242.
54 Ibid., fol. 18, Ganong to Walker, 10 November 1916.
55 Ibid., Langton to Walker, 18 November 1916.
56 Ibid., Walker to Biggar, 23 November 1916. This "introduction" was the only major essay included in The Champlain Society edition of the *Works*, vol. 1 (Toronto, 1922): 193–202. After all the years it was written, it is still "an excellent piece of work."
57 Ibid., fol. 19, Walker to Biggar, 6 June 1917.
58 *Rules for the Guidance of Editors of Publications of the Champlain Society* (Toronto: The Champlain Society, 1915).
59 Ibid., fol. 11, Ganong to Walker, 16 October 1915.
60 Ibid., fol. 12, 12 November; fol, 15, 29 April; fol, 16, 22 December 1916.

suggested to Walker that the inclusion of all these maps in the books would break their spines and that they should think of a map portfolio.[61]

Shortly after Biggar had begun his editorial work, the pressing matter of the 62 plates that accompanied the *Brief Discours* arose again. By this time it was known that all were in colour. On March 9, 1915, Langton wrote to the John Carter Brown Library to get permission to reproduce them.[62] The press chosen for a price estimate was the Heliotype Co., Boston. On March 18, Walker received a quote that their best colour process on high-grade paper applied to the 62 plates for 500 copies was $7,627, and for 1000 copies, $8,243. Cheaper processes on cheaper paper resulted in $7,097 and $7,750.50 for 500 and 1000 copies, and a bottom-line process, $5,878 and $6,756 for 500 and 1000 copies.[63] Shocked at the price of the Heliotype quotes Walker reviewed the project with William V. Kellen of the Brown Library who offered to get him a quote from another company.[64] The company chosen was the Wright Illustration and Engraving Co. of Boston, but preferring not to send these unique illustrations out, Kellen, on suggestion from the management of the library, requested that the photos are to be taken at the library.[65] He did however lend one plate to the Wright Engraving Co. for reproduction. The colour proofs of this illustration, on three different types of paper, reached Langton in December but were judged to be of inferior quality.[66] Walker now suggested that in view of the cost, the illustrations be done in black and white with one in colour by Heliotype.[67] The library however would no longer let any of the manuscript illustrations out and would only co-operate further if the illustrations were photographed in the library.[68] In February, cost estimates came from Heliotype and Wright Engraving. Heliotype quoted $335 for 1000 copies of one colour plate, and $23.50 for 1000 copies of one black and white print, while Wright quoted $132.41 for 1000 copies of one colour plate.[69] But Wright was no longer in the running and Heliotype was given the contract to do the black and white reproductions.[70] Proofs for the black and whites arrived in August,[71] but debate over how many colour illustrations to include lingered on. In September a quote from Heliotype arrived for four colour

---

61 Ibid., fol. 16, Biggar to Walker, 10 May 1917.
62 Ibid., fol. 9, Langton to Winship (Brown Librarian), 9 March 1915.
63 Ibid., Heliotype to Langton, 26 May 1915.
64 Ibid., fol. 10, Walker to Kellen, 20 September; Kellen to Walker, 24 September 1915.
65 Ibid., fol. 12, Kellen to Walker, 29 November 1915.
66 Ibid., Wright Engraving to Langton, 6, 14 and 20 December 1915. The three colour proofs are with the letter of 6 December. They are of Plate XII, *St. Iovan De Porteticot* (Island of Porto Rico). The cost of reproducing this plate in colour was $56.70. Ibid., item 15, General ledger 1906–1962, Acct. # 38.
67 Ibid., Walker to Kellen, 16 December 1905.
68 Ibid., Kellen to Walker, 20 January 1916, and fol. 13, February 7.
69 Ibid., fol. 14, Heliotype, 12 February 1916; fol. 13, Wright Engraving, 18 February 1916.
70 Ibid., Langton to Ramsey (Heliotype), 8 June 1916.
71 Ibid., Heliotype to Langton, 17 August 1916.

plates at $600 for 500 copies and $675 for 1000.[72] The plan to include one or more colour plates was finally put to rest in mid 1922, after the first volume had gone to press.[73] This late date accounts for the statement, prematurely published by Biggar in his introduction to the *Works* thanking the Committee of Management at the John Carter Brown Library for the "exceptional privilege" of permitting the "reproductions in colour…of the sixty-two illustrations reproduced in the portfolio."[74] Months after the Society members had received their copy of the first volume, some were still writing letters to the secretary asking where their colour plates were.

In addition to his problems with Ganong, Biggar ran into an unexpected one with Cultru's corrections of Laverdière's text. When he compared Cultru's revisions to an original of *Des Sauvages* at the British Museum (now in the British Library) he found that Cultru had made a number of errors. Biggar made the necessary corrections and sent them to the press for inclusion, an expensive process since the text had already been typeset. Now distrustful of the Laverdière/Cultru collation, Biggar purchased a photocopy of *Des Sauvages* from the British Library for £2/10/0, and used an original volume he owned to check *Les Voyages, 1613*.[75] A further blow came ten months later, in January 1918, when Biggar was notified that Cultru had died early the previous year and had only managed to collate the *Brief Discours*, *Des Sauvages* and the beginning of *Les Voyages, 1613*.[76] Biggar now reversed himself on the need for a Francophone collator and suggested that Professor J. Home Cameron, then head of the University of Toronto French Department, be contacted to proofread the Laverdière texts against the originals, a proposition with which Walker agreed.[77] Since Cultru's fee for collating the first volume had been $60, Cameron was asked to collate the next five volumes for $300. To save costs he was to use only original editions located in Canada and that "if he needs something in Paris it can be photographed and sent him."[78] It was agreed that there was practically nothing for Cameron to do on the first volume.[79] Walker finally heard from Cameron on July 10, that he would undertake the work but not until the following summer (1919) owing to a heavy teaching schedule.[80] Thus finally, eleven years after the project began, someone with expertise in Champlain's French had been found to collate the original texts.

---

72 Ibid., Heliotype to Champlain Society, 4 September 1916.
73 MS Coll. 1, box 10, Hanson to Walker, 19 June 1922. R.W. Hanson, Director of Spottiswoode Press, suggested that the plans for doing colour illustrations be dropped because they were too expensive.
74 Biggar, ed. *Works*, vol. I, p. xvii.
75 MS Coll. 50, box 48, fol. 19, Biggar to Walker, 17 March 1917.
76 Ibid., fol. 20, Biggar to walker, 2 January 1918.
77 Ibid., Walker to Biggar, 18 January 1918.
78 Ibid., Biggar to Langton, 5 July 1918.
79 MS Coll. 1, box 14, Walker to Biggar, 1 June 1919.
80 MS Coll. 50, box 48, fol. 21, Cameron to Walker, 10 July 1918.

The length of time it took to edit Champlain's *Works* would inevitably have repercussions among the printers. Ballantyne's had gone into liquidation in the spring of 1916 and became Spottiswoode, Ballantyne and Co. In December 1917, Spottiswoode wanted a commitment on layout, paper and other matters because the price of printing was rising due to the war.[81] By May, the following year, R.W. Hanson, director of the press, wrote that the price of paper of the type specified by Walker had risen about 300%, "if it is still made," and so had type setting, binding, cost of reproductions, labour and storage of the type already set. He hoped that he would receive the final proofs before everything goes up again in price, and sensibly suggested reducing the number of volumes and raising membership fees. Alternatively, Hanson advised the Society that they might delay publishing until after the war, but in the end he argued against it because there was no assurance that prices would go down again.[82] In this matter Biggar argued against the press and suggested that publication be delayed until paper prices returned to earlier levels.[83] It is also probable that the delay urged by Biggar was because he was not nearly ready to go to press. Most of Champlain's books had been translated and partially edited but none except the texts that were to go into the first volume had been proofread.[84] A letter by Walker to Spottiswoode in June effectively put the printing part of the project on hold. He suggested that when the press received the proofs for the first Champlain volume and "Wood's War," the texts be type set, plates moulded and placed in storage; and further, that the paper that had already been purchased for the two volumes be sold, it was hoped at a profit.[85]

As 1919 wore on, Walker's direct participation in the Champlain project began to wane. Increasingly Hugh Langton handled all matters pertaining to the press and with Biggar, the sub-editors and translators. Professor John Squair, recently retired from the University of Toronto French Department, was asked to proofread more of the French text and Ganong the maps.[86]

With the arrival of summer 1919, Cameron departed for Québec to begin collation of the 1619 and 1632 *Voyages*, only to discover that the Legislative Library was closed for holidays in July and August.[87] He seems then to have examined the handwritten transcription of *Des Sauvages* in the Bibliothèque du Séminaire de Québec, that had been used by Laverdière for his *Œuvres,* and discovered that it had many errors. His

---

81 Ibid., fol. 19, Spottiswoode to Walker, 21 December 1917.
82 Ibid., fol. 20, Hanson to Walker, 10 May 1918.
83 Ibid., Biggar to Walker, 24 May 1918.
84 Ibid.
85 Ibid., Walker to Hanson, 6 June 1918. "Wood's War" referred to here, was the first of four volumes on *The Canadian War of 1812* (Toronto: The Champlain Society, 1920) being edited by Col. William Wood. The others followed in 1923, 1927 and 1928.
86 Ibid., fol. 22, Langton to Biggar, 18 December 1919; fol. 23, Biggar to Langton, 1 January 1920; Langton to Squair, 29 January 1920; Biggar to Langton, 30 April 1920.
87 Ibid., fol. 22, Cameron to Langton, 12 September 1919.

comment is an example of the kind he wrote on the margins of all the Laverdière texts as he began to correct them:

> The MS copy (calligraphic) in the Laverdière Library cannot be accurate. The copyist follows his own fancy, apparently, in reproducing or rather changing Caps to small letters, in inserting n and m in nasal contractions and doubtless in many other ways, especially in putting accents which are evidently not in the original. They are rare in the 1619 and 1620 editions. As an example take the last words in the work [i.e. *Des Sauvages*]: *Haure de Grace*, which he writes *Hâvre-de-Grâce*.[88]

By December, Cameron had gone over Cultru's "corrections" of Laverdière and reported that this work as well had: "…omissions or misapplications of accents, the nasal sign instead of the letter 'n'…which Laverdière ignored…" with the query, "should he go over it?"[89] If the answer was affirmative, there would be yet another delay with Volume One, but whatever Langton or Biggar thought, the Council of the Champlain Society ruled that the text should be exact and that decided the matter. The French texts for the *Brief Discours* and *Des Sauvages*, which were thought to be finished, and in galley stage now underwent a new collation. Langton, who had translated the two books, also thought he was reading the galleys for the last time only to discover that Biggar had made changes to his translation of *Des Sauvages*. Where Champlain used the word *salubre* to describe what the Algonquins had told him about the water of Lakes Erie and Ontario, Langton translated the word as "fresh" and "wholesome." Biggar however had changed his translation to "brackish" and "salty." Biggar's reasons were that Bourne (1906), following Purchas (1625) had used "salty" and "brackish," and that Champlain probably meant brackish "… for so the word is translated in Purchas."[90] A frustrated Langton fired back that he could not find any "linguistical authority" that would render *salubre* as "brackish," and that the derivation of the word is from the Latin *salubris*, meaning "healthful" and "wholesome."[91] Unfortunately Langton lost the argument with the result that several generations of Anglophone readers of the *Works* are under the impression that the Algonquins described the Great Lakes to Champlain as being salty.

During this time Langton, as treasurer of the Society also had to cope with Spottiswoode. In 1918, the paper for the impending volumes had been sold and in the spring of 1920 Langton had to order a new stock, thinking that the first volume would

---

88 Ibid., box 47. Note written by Cameron (Québec, 1919) on the back of the title page of his photocopy of *Des Sauvages* [n.d.]. In the printed version Laverdière gives the spelling of the port as it is in the original, *Haure de Grace*.
89 Ibid., Langton to Biggar, 18 December 1919.
90 Ibid., fol. 24, Biggar to Langton, 10 May 1920.
91 Ibid., Langton to Biggar, 29 May. In October 1918, Ganong had similar arguments with Biggar who had changed Ganong's translation of *barque* from "pinnace" to "longboat" when the context clearly demanded a larger vessel than a longboat.

be ready for printing by the summer.[92] A month later, he got word from Hanson at the press that paper was in short supply and there would be a four-month's delay in getting the stock. Furthermore, they had to know how many copies of the book would be printed.[93] Hanson also pointed out that the 62 illustrations he had received for the *Brief Discours*, 1200 copies of each, were all at different scales, which should be mentioned in the introduction to the book. This led to a decision by the Society to print the size of the originals (height x width) beneath each of the images.[94] To do that, they had to track down the original photos which were with Cameron on holidays somewhere near Beaumaris on Lake Muskoka, which caused yet another delay.[95] In reply to Hanson's query regarding the number of copies for which to order paper, Langton must have replied that the plan was to publish 550 copies of the first volume. This prompted a letter from Walker asking him to correct that to 1200 copies.[96] This letter was followed by a memo specifying a press run for 1150 books: members, 500; National Battlefields Commission, 100; review purposes, 20; public edition, 600; surplus, 30. Of these 550 were to be printed immediately.[97] Walker at least, still had an edition for the public in mind. In fact, in October 1916, The Champlain Society had asked Burrows Bros. of Cleveland, Ohio, the press that had published the 73-volume edition of the *Jesuit Relations* under the editorship of Reuben Gold Thwaites, if they would act as the distributor of the Champlain volumes intended for the public. When Burrows Bros. declined because their Old and Rare Books Department had been discontinued, Arthur H. Clark Co., also of Cleveland, was approached.[98]

Early in October 1920, with Spottiswoode ready to print, the final proofs for Volume One had not yet been received from Cameron; "What is the matter with him…I have not had a line from him for a whole year," was the cry of a frustrated Biggar.[99] Unfortunately Cameron had found more errors in Cultru's text and had to make "a great many changes," among them a better translation of the title page from *On Savages* to *Of Savages*.[100] Langton now took the opportunity brought by Cameron's revisions to

---

92   Ibid., fol. 23, Langton to Ganong, 24 April 1920.
93   Ibid., fol. 24, Hanson to Langton, 19 March 1920.
94   MS Coll. 1, box 14, Walker to Langton, 23 June 1920.
95   MS Coll. 50, box 48, fol. 24, Langton to Stennet, 23 June 1920. Alice E. Stennet was executive secretary treasurer of the Champlain Society from 1919–24. She was preceded by Eleanor Creighton (1905–13) and was followed by Julia Jarvis.
96   Ibid., fol. 25, Walker to Langton, 13 August 1920.
97   Ibid., Stennet to Langton, 25 August 1920.
98   Ibid., fol. 17, Langton to Burrows Bros., 11 October 1916; fol. 18, Burrows Bros. to Langton, 6 November 1916; Langton to Arthur H. Clark, 10 November 1916. No answer from Arthur H. Clark has been located in MS Coll. 50.
99   Ibid., fol. 25, Biggar to Langton, 30 October 1920.
100 Ibid., Langton to Biggar, 22 November 1920.

admit to Biggar that some words he had translated in *Des Sauvages* "baffled" him and to take his translations merely as suggestions:

> Can one translate *Barque* [a type of ship] by "bark"? *Canot* by "canoe"? *Chaloupe* by "shallop or sloop"? *Patache* in English "patache"? *Sapin* should be "spruce", not "fir" since fir is "a bookish word"? *Noyer* is probably the "butternut", certainly not "walnut", it is given once or twice as "nut bearing tree." The term "wigwam or tent" is used for Native structures, not "lodge, hut or cabin."[101]

Early in December 1920, Biggar obtained a photostat of an "unknown" 1604 edition of *Des Sauvages* from the Bibliothéque Nationale, Paris,[102] and began to check it against the undated version. He then sent it to Cameron for comment. That this 1604 edition was "discovered" so late and was believed to be "the only copy in existence" is astonishing.[103] Had a feasibility study of the project been undertaken, the 1604 printing of *Des Sauvages* would surely have been "discovered." In his Preface to the Prince Society translation of the *Voyages* (1880), well known to The Champlain Society editors, Charles Pomeroy Otis noted that he had used a 1604 original in the Harvard Library.[104] Furthermore, a publication to which some Champlain Society editors and consultants such as William Ganong, Charles Colby and George Wrong had contributed chapters, contained a "Notes bibliographiques..." listing the 1604 Harvard original as well as a second 1604 original that had been sold at auction in New York in 1907.[105] While Cameron was doing his check of the 1604 edition, the press was asking for the "final" proofs of the first volume.[106] Shortly thereafter Biggar received more corrections from Cameron as a result of seeing the 1604 text. At first Biggar could not fathom why there should be so many more corrections to *Des Sauvages*. When he had checked the undated text he had found only "four differences" between it and the 1604 printing. Eventually it dawned on Biggar that "Cameron has gone on the assumption that the text should be a facsimile, which it was never intended to be...I have merely aimed at a correct text."[107] Was it now worth the expense to make the changes at this late date? When Hanson at Spottiswoode received Cameron's changes he suggested that they simply ignore them

---

101 Ibid., Langton to Biggar, 3 December 1920.
102 Ibid., Biggar to Langton, 7 December 1920.
103 Ibid., box 47, Cameron's notes with the Photostat of the 1604 edition clearly indicate that he thought the Paris original to be the only copy in existence. See also *The Works*, ed., Biggar, vol. I: xvii.
104 Champlain, *Voyages of Samuel de Champlain*, ed. Slafter, trans. Otis, vol. 1: 215.
105 Philéas Gagnon, "Notes bibliographiques sur les écrits de Champlain, manuscrits et imprimés," *Bulletin de la Sociéte de Géographie de Québec: Á Champlain, 1608–1908* (Juillet, 1908): 55–77; in particular, 60–62. Both the [n.d.] edition and the 1604 were also noted by Narcisse E. Dionne, *Champlain*, (Makers of Canada Series, Toronto: Morang & Co. 1906): 14–15.
106 MS Coll. 50, box 48, fol. 26, Hanson (Spottiswoode) to Langton, 24 February 1921.
107 Ibid., Biggar to Langton, 26 February 1921. While Biggar was pouring out his frustrations about Cameron to Langton, the latter was receiving similar letters marked "Personal and Confidential" from Cameron about Biggar; see: 21 March 1921.

and start printing because the corrections required "recompositioning" the first eighty pages at a cost of £40.[108] After "a hot discussion" Langton and the Council of the Society were of the opinion that the text be reproduced exactly, initiating yet another delay.[109] This drew an expected response from Biggar who must have felt that his position as general editor was being undermined:

> The method we have followed is that adopted by the editors of the Société de l'Histoire de France. I have therefore no intention of altering the present method, of which not only Cultru approved, but which has also satisfied such critics as La Roncière and Foulché-Delbosc. At present I am going through the proofs, adopting as many of Cameron's suggestions as possible. I have no intention however of putting commas in wrong places nor of writing *il y a* because the original happens to have these.[110]

Having received these comments, Langton suggested to Biggar that he should have outlined his editorial principles in the Introduction to the volume, and enquired whether it was not too late to do so.[111] On August 5, 1921 Hanson confirmed that he would print 550 copies of the book and suggested printing 1150 copies of each of the maps and illustrations for £249, which would save £61 when the popular printing went into production.[112] This suggestion was accepted. Two more incidents caused yet another delay. The wrong negative of the 1607 map had been sent to the printer and the proofreader at Spottiswoode had made changes "at his own sweet will."[113] Biggar now had to go over the galleys again and in a parting shot asked Langton if he and Ganong had ever read the *Rules for Editors* the Society had printed in 1915, since they did not seem to follow them; to which Langton pointedly replied that he had forgotten them since he had done his editing such a long time ago.[114] Biggar was more conciliatory with Cameron, writing him a letter in which he thanked him for his work.[115]

On December 22, 1921, Hanson reported that Biggar had cleared the texts and that they would start printing shortly.[116] On 27 June, the following year, 5 cases, containing 430 books were sent on the steamer *Varentia* to Canada. The copies for the English members were sent directly from the press and another 50 were held for later

---

108 Ibid., Hanson to Langton, 30 March 1921.
109 Ibid., Langton to Biggar, 12 July 1921.
110 Ibid., Langton to Cameron (quoting Biggar), 8 August 1921.
111 Ibid., Langton to Biggar, 8 August 1921. On 25 July Biggar had cabled Langton that "Cameron better send a short introduction." Langton was right; this was Biggar's responsibility, not Cameron's. Biggar did in fact write a short introduction dated 8 June 1921, which says little about editorial principals of either the French or English texts. Champlain, *The Works*, ed., Biggar, vol. 1(1922): xiii–xviii.
112 Ibid., Hanson to Langton, 5 August 1921.
113 Ibid., Biggar to Langton, 7 December 1921. The right copy of the 1607 map finally arrived 15 February 1922, fol. 27, Biggar to Langton
114 Ibid., Biggar to Langton, 7 December 1921; Langton to Biggar, 20 December 1921.
115 Ibid., Biggar to Cameron, 9 November 1921.
116 Ibid., Hanson to Stennet, 22 December 1921.

shipment.[117] Walker had been sent an advance copy of the book and the portfolio of maps, with which he "was greatly satisfied."[118] When the books arrived they were held in customs until a sales tax of $295.00 had been paid. An appeal resulted in a rebate of $79.44.[119]

The final printing costs from Spottiswoode for Volume I, with the portfolio of maps, was $5,151.78; the illustrations from Heliotype were $1,864.73; the editorial fees $600.00,[120] and other expenses $624.25,[121] for a staggering total of $8240.76, far in excess of the original estimates. By contrast, the average cost of the thirteen volumes published in the Regular Series before 1922 was $1,903.70 (see Tables 3 a, and 4).[122]

The irritations caused by the long drawn out process of getting the first volume into print were of course exacerbated by its hideous cost. Unfortunately no one had foreseen the difficulties that would be caused by Champlain's language and the complex printing history of the texts, and the supposedly "near perfect" Lavèrdiere edition blinded them to the necessity of preparing a new collation. That a new collation of the texts was necessary did not strike the Society until five years after the project started and even then no estimates were made of the length of time it might take to make a thorough collation. Not until the volume was well underway did anyone make an inventory of the number and size of Champlain's illustrations and the reproduction cost of these. There were no definitive editorial policies on how to render the text and footnotes. The haste in getting the volume printed led to premature type setting, revisions and added costs while the location of the press in England and wartime conditions led to increased material and shipping costs. Many of these problems should have been foreseen.

Even if this had been a problem free production, it would have been an expensive one. This is without a doubt the most complex book the Society ever published. The text was the product of five scholars, Langton, Ganong, Cultru, Cameron and Biggar. The portfolio contained three large maps and 62 reproductions of Champlain's drawings, and the book itself, sixteen reproductions of Champlain's smaller maps, twenty-five sketch maps by Ganong and five photographic facsimiles.

The irritating delay in getting the volume into the hands of the members was also aggravated by the slow production of the other volumes. Of the 26 volumes that had been accepted before and during the twelve years from 1911 to 1922 and that were still underway, nine volumes had appeared in print, but there were five years when no

---

117 Ibid., fol. 28, Hanson to Stennet, 26 June 1922.
118 Ibid.
119 Ibid., fol. 29, August 14 and December 12, 1922.
120 Ibid., box 49, fol. 1, Biggar to Wrong, 16 November 1922. Editorial fees were allocated as follows: Langton $100; Cultru $53.21; Ganong $100; Biggar $246.79, and a "bonus" of $100 voted to him the following year; fol. 2, 20 February 1922.
121 Includes items such as, taxes, freight, insurance, photos, cables, storage, etc.
122 Ibid., item 15, General Ledger 1906–1962, Acct. # 38.

volume appeared, only two years that saw two volumes and seven projected volumes that were cancelled (Table 2 b). Of the cancelled volumes, McLennan's *Louisbourg* was actually finished but considered to be too long. After unpleasant arguments McLennan refused to cut back the length of the text and number of illustrations and published his book elsewhere.[123] The projected volume on *Sir Charles Bagot's Papers* by Edward Kylie was near completion but needed revisions and extensive editing. It was cancelled in 1916, the year Kylie died.[124] The *Explorations by Petitot* was cancelled for unknown reasons. The editor C.D. Melville had translated the first ten chapters the *Grand Lac Des Ours* needing only the last two chapters to complete the text.[125] Nothing remains of the projected *Clergy Reserves* volume except a notation that J.P. Laycock had been paid a $250 advance.

Clearly, what was needed for future proposals was a more careful screening of potential editors, careful estimates of volume content, time commitments and potential costs. As for the remaining Champlain volumes, a realistic estimate had to be made how the process of collating the texts could be speeded up and costs cut back.

EDITING THE LATER VOLUMES

VOLUME II, 1922 TO 1925

By the time Volume I appeared, fourteen years had elapsed since the project officially began. Although most of the effort during these years went into completing the first volume, the other volumes were in various states of advancement.

Originally Biggar had wanted the second Champlain volume, containing Book II of *Les Voyages, 1613* (1608–1612) and the *Quatriesme Voyage* (1613) to be translated and edited by Ganong using Grant's revisions of the text by Otis, which had been published by the Prince Society.[126] Ganong however, was busy translating and editing Chrestien Le Clercq's *New Relation of Gaspesia*[127] and felt he was not familiar enough with areas

---

123 John S. McLennan, *Louisbourg: From Its Foundation to Its Fall, 1713–1758* (Toronto: Macmillan, 1918). This volume is still considered to be a good starting point for a study of the fortress.
124 MS Coll. 50, box 53, contains the entire manuscript. For his work to the date of cancellation Kylie had been paid $284.00. Kylie (1881–1916) was an associate professor of modern history at the U. of T., a protégé of George Wrong and knew Sir Edmund Walker through the Round Table movement. He died of typhoid and pneumonia in 1616. Ramsey Cook, "Kylie, Edward Joseph," *Dictionary of Canadian Biography, Vol. 14, 1911–1920* (Toronto: University of Toronto Press, 1998).
125 Ibid., box 45, fol. 8–36. There is no explanation of who Melville was. The address he gave was at Meole Hall, Shrewsbury, England. Included with the manuscript translation are 36 photographs of scenery, Natives, log cabins and the ruins of a building that may have been a trading post. There are no captions on the photos.
126 Ibid., box 27, fol. 7, Biggar to Wrong, 26 March 1909. Champlain, *Voyages of Samuel de Champlain, 1604–1618*. ed. Grant.
127 Chrestien Le Clercq, *New Relation of Gaspesia with the Customs and Religion of the Gaspesian Indians by Father Chrestien Le Clercq*, ed. William F. Ganong (Toronto: The Champlain Society, 1910). This was

outside Acadia.¹²⁸ Grant was of course a logical choice, but had fallen behind in editing the second and third volumes of Lescarbot. There the fate of Volume II rested until Langton raised it again in a letter to Biggar late in 1919 suggesting that Professor John Squair of the University of Toronto French Department¹²⁹ (Figure 10) undertake the translations for Volume II, with Cameron to collate the French text.¹³⁰ Biggar concurred and suggested Squair use Grant's revisions of the Otis' translation as a guide.¹³¹ In his letter to Squair, requesting the translation, Langton did not mention Walker's opinion about Grant, but wrote rather disingenuously that "Grant was too busy" to do it himself.¹³² By the end of April, Squair had agreed to prepare the translation for $150.¹³³

Squair worked quickly and on 4 October 1921 submitted his completed text and collected $150 plus $40 for typing costs.¹³⁴ By February the following year, Biggar had begun to read Squair's text which he judged to be "…dull and not too accurate," and expressed the hope that Squair could take criticism.¹³⁵ Upon further investigation he noted that Squair merely translated Laverdière's notes rather than supplying his own.¹³⁶ This situation lingered for a year until Stewart Wallace¹³⁷ (Figure 11), newly appointed as general editor to replace George Wrong, contacted Biggar, who was on a visit to Ottawa, in order to reach a decision on the Squair manuscript. They agreed that Squair's notes were "insufficient, unoriginal and inaccurate," but, as Wallace explained, the reason that Squair would not supply notes on matters of "historical and geographical character" was because he knew "comparatively little about those matters." ¹³⁸ Biggar suggested that he could compose the notes providing he was paid for them.¹³⁹ Without getting into money matters Wallace concurred that Biggar himself could do them, or perhaps Grant.¹⁴⁰ Knowing that Grant was no option, Biggar sensed that he was going to

---

the fifth Society volume.
128 Ibid., fol. 17, Ganong to Wrong, 8 April 1908; Ganong to Wrong, 17 May 1909.
129 John Squair (1850–1928) was head of the University of Toronto French Department until 1916 when he retired. His successor as head was J. Home Cameron. Squair had authored a number of French textbooks and been a member of the Champlain Society since its inception.
130 Ibid., box 48, fol. 22, Langton to Biggar, 18 December 1919. Unlike the later volumes, *Les Voyages…1613* appeared in only one edition and therefore presented fewer problems in collating the French text.
131 Ibid., fol. 23, Biggar to Langton, 1 January 1920.
132 Ibid., Langton to Squair, 29 January 1920.
133 Ibid., Biggar to Langton, 30 April 1920.
134 Ibid., item 15, General Ledger 1906–1962, Acct. # 38.
135 Ibid., box 48, fol. 27, Biggar to Langton, 15 February 1922.
136 Ibid., box 49, fol. 1, Biggar to Langton. 15 March 1922.
137 William Stewart Wallace was a historian and chief librarian at the University of Toronto from 1923 to 1954. A scholar with extensive editorial experience he served as general editor of the Champlain Society (1923–43), president (1943–48) and honorary president (1963–70).
138 MS Col. 50, box 49, fol. 2, Wallace to Biggar, 9 January 1923.
139 Ibid., Biggar to Wallace, 12 January 1923.
140 Ibid., fol. 2, Wallace to Biggar, 16 January 1923.

Figure 10. John Squair. Professor of French, University of Toronto, 1901–16. Photo about 1916.

Figure 11. William Stewart Wallace. Chief Librarian, University of Toronto (1923–54). General Editor for the Champlain Society (1923–43; 1949–52) and President (1943–8). Photo about 1918.

be asked to do the job in spite of the fact that he had been complaining for years about all the work he was asked to do for next to no remuneration. Claiming that he had spent ten years on the first volume for £50 he was not about to write and revise Squair's notes for nothing.[141] Following this letter Biggar pointed out that the Society still owed him £2 for cables and $1.65 for illustrations.[142] Pleading that the Society was "in poor financial shape," which was not really true (see Table 4– Balance current account, 1923 and 1924), Wallace tried to delay, but a week later, probably after speaking with Wrong and Walker, Biggar received a payment for the cables and illustrations ($11.65) as well as a bonus of $100 for completing Volume I and $150 on account for Volume II.[143]

By the end of March 1923, the manuscript text for Volume II had been reworked by Biggar and retyped by the Society's new secretary, Julia Jarvis (Figure 12), for $44[144]. Biggar however, found that "her mistakes and omissions have given me a great deal of unnecessary trouble."[145] Through the spring and summer, Cameron was collating the French text using an original text owned by Biggar.[146] On Dominion Day (July 1, 1923) Biggar arrived in Pembroke, Ontario, to give a Dominion Day address and to see the portage taken by Champlain in 1613 on his visit to chief Tessoüat on Morrison Island. It was on this portage that Champlain allegedly lost his astrolabe.[147] Rental of a motor launch to Morrison Island had cost $20 and the six pictures taken by a photographer hired to go along cost another $18. When the Society was confronted with the invoices they balked, even though Biggar included two more illustrations free of charge. Of these, one was a photo of the astrolabe, given to him by its owner Samuel V. Hoffman of New Jersey, and the other, a map of Champlain's route, a gift from Mr. J. L. Morris of Pembroke who had requested Biggar's presence at the Dominion Day ceremonies. Reimbursement to Biggar was eventually reduced to $32 since two of the six Morrison Island photos were duplicates.[148]

The English and French texts for Volume II were sent to Spottiswoode in the late summer and on 28 September Wallace forwarded the galley proofs to Biggar, Squair and Cameron for checking.[149] Thinking that the proofs were in more or less final form,

---

141 Ibid., Biggar to Wallace, 18 January 1923.
142 Ibid., Biggar to Wallace, 3 February 1923.
143 Ibid., Wallace to Biggar, 12 February 1923; Wrong to Biggar, 20 February 1923; Stennet to Walker, 20 February 1923; Wallace to Wrong, 20 February 1923; fol. 3. Biggar to Stennet, 26 February 1923.
144 Ibid., fol. 12, Langton to Walker, 25 May 1923.
145 Ibid., fol. 13, Biggar to Wallace, 4 July 1923.
146 Ibid., Biggar to Wallace, 7 August 1923.
147 Douglas Hunter, "The Mystery of Champlain's Astrolabe." *The Beaver* (December 2004 / January 2005): 14–23.
148 MS Col. 50, box 49, fol. 3, Biggar to Wallace, 8 September 1923. The photographer was from "Artona Studio," 68 Pembroke St., Pembroke, Ontario. Ibid., item 15, General Ledger 1906–1962, entry for 8 October.
149 Ibid., fol. 4, Wallace to Biggar, 28 September 1923.

Figure 12. Julia Jarvis. Executive Secretary, The Champlain Society, Toronto (1924–59).

Wallace informed Council of the likelihood that Volume II would appear in the spring of 1924.[150] Squair's corrections were sent to Biggar on October 12, who received them at the end of the month.[151] All eyes were now on Cameron who assured Wallace that he was "…working on the final revision of it [the French text] now, and comparing the translation with it, so as to eliminate some of the notes, and better adapt those which remained."[152] Unfortunately, he could not promise a completion date. The fact that Cameron was also checking Squair's translation, which the others had thought to be problematic, but with Biggar's work passable, should have been a signal to expect a lengthy delay. On 19 January 1924, Biggar sent word to Wallace that he had received nothing from Cameron and had started on Langton's translations for Volume III.[153] Early in February, both Wallace and Biggar, who were increasingly desperate to meet the publication deadline, sent letters to Cameron asking where his texts were for Volume II.[154]

While in the throes of moving Volume II ahead, Sir Edmund Walker died on 27 March 1924, aged 75. The following morning the headline in the Toronto Globe read:

> A GIANT OAK HAS FALLEN AND ALL CANADA MOURNS LOSS OF GREAT NATIVE SON…Possibly no more versatile Canadian existed in his day and age; probably few others have done so much for Canada.

Activities in the Champlain Society were halted temporarily as, fittingly, Professor George Wrong assumed the Presidency on April 16. Stewart Wallace remained secretary and general editor and Hugh H. Langton remained treasurer. Both had been appointed the previous year.

Early in April, while Biggar was still waiting for Cameron, he wrote that he had found a number of hitherto unknown Champlain documents that he wanted to send to Squair for translation to be included in Volume II.[155] Wallace, reporting back to Biggar, wrote that Squair was unable to undertake the translation of the documents and as far as Cameron was concerned, "I have done everything to stir him up, but he is so slow and so meticulous that it seems impossible to hurry him."[156] By mid May the first small batch of Cameron's corrected galleys reached Biggar and in mid June he received the rest with the news from Wallace that Professor Louis Allen at the University of Toronto French Department was translating the additional documents for Squair. Wallace added that he hoped that Volume II would be out in September or

---

150 Ibid., Wallace to Biggar, 10 October 1923; Ibid., Item 65, Minutes of 28 September 1923.
151 Ibid., fol. 4, Wallace to Biggar, 12 October 1923; Biggar to Wallace, 30 October 1923.
152 Ibid., Cameron to Wallace, 12 November 1923.
153 Ibid., fol. 5, Biggar to Wallace, 19 January 1924.
154 Ibid., Wallace to Cameron, 1 February 1924; Biggar to Wallace, 12 February 1924.
155 Ibid., Biggar to Wallace, 7 April 1924.
156 Ibid., Wallace to Biggar, 24 April 1924.

October, but Biggar thought a distribution date for February would be more realistic.[157] On June 16, Allen finished the documents and Wallace wrote Biggar that Volume II must be out before the end of the year or there would be no book for the membership in 1924.[158] By late September, when the corrected English galleys were with the printer to be turned into page proofs, Wrong received letters from Ganong complaining of the scholarship that had gone into Volume II. Evidently he had been sent a set of the galleys for comment. In his opinion it was "regrettable" that the notes to Volume II were not "more thorough by someone who knows the area and so forth"; the volume, he added, promised to be not much of an advance over Otis, Slafter and Laverdière.[159] It may be recalled that Ganong had turned down the task of annotating the volume, claiming a lack of knowledge about the St. Lawrence region.

During the Council meeting of October 2, George Wrong was instructed to write to the National Battlefields Commission for the second half of the grant ($2,500), awarded on April 6, 1909. At the same meeting the announcement was made that Volume II would be delayed because Biggar had decided to add new material to the volume.[160] This led to a highly critical letter to Biggar by Langton in his capacity as treasurer of the Society: that Council was "sorry to learn" of the delay; that it was "a pity" that he included documents in this volume that should have been left to a volume on documents; that Council had considered such a "documentary appendix" which was now no longer possible due to the inclusion of documents in a regular volume; that the extra documents "have no particular relevancy" except for the date; that Champlain's marriage contract [one of the new documents] was not translated properly, has too many legal phrases and should not have been included in full. In short, he hoped there was still time to withdraw the documents and ordered that in the future, to keep costs down, Council must first clear the inclusion of extra documents and their cost. On a happier note, Langton let Biggar know that he had his part of Volume III finished and was waiting for the collated text from Cameron.[161] It took Biggar almost a month to reply: he felt he had not exceeded his authority as general editor to include the documents; that Champlain's marriage contract is important because it was one of the few items in existence about his family life; that he did not know that there was "great urgency" to get the volume out in 1924 and felt that the real "stumbling block" was not the addition of the documents but Cameron's slow responses. He did agree that in future he would clear potential costs with Council.[162] He might have added that he had informed Wallace, the general editor of the Society, as early as April 7 that he had found

---

157 Ibid., Biggar to Wallace, 8 May, 14 May, and 20 May 1924; Wallace to Biggar, 2 June and 12 June 1924.
158 Ibid., fol. 6, Wallace to Biggar, 16 June and 4 July 1924.
159 Ibid., box 39, Ganong to Wrong, 26 September and 11 October 1924.
160 Ibid., item 65, Minutes of 2 October 1924.
161 Ibid., box 49, fol. 6, Langton to Biggar, 7 October 1924.
162 Ibid., Biggar to Langton, 1 November 1924.

new documents and that it was Wallace who had sent them to Allen for translation on June 2. The suggestion that Council had been considering a "documentary appendix" must have struck Biggar as bizarre since Council had refused to approve just such a volume in 1911.[163] Understandably Biggar felt that he should not be blamed entirely for the delays since he was still waiting for Cameron's collated French text for Volume II.[164]

Biggar now presented Langton with a list of illustrations he wanted to include in Volume II.[165] This led to an explosion from Langton. He offered to "go after the French text from Cameron" but the list of pictures "is the first intimation we have had of illustrations to the volume." He pointed out again that Council had to know of all expenses beforehand and that pages would be cut from the book if the cost of the illustrations were too high. This admonition was followed by a long explanation of deficits faced by the Society and yet again, that no added expenses were to be "incurred except by resolution of Council."[166] In finishing the letter Biggar was told to cut the picture of Henri de Bourbon, Prince de Condé "as his physiognomy is not vital for the understanding of Champlain."[167] A month later Biggar responded that he still had nothing from Cameron. By way of explanation for not consulting about the list of illustrations he noted quite correctly that he had always done that with Sir Edmund who had always approved them and that he was adamant about including Condé who adds only £2 to the total costs of the volume.[168] As for Council and Langton not knowing about the illustrations, Langton must have forgotten that he discussed at least three of the illustrations with Ganong a year earlier as well as having paid for the photos of Morrison Island.[169] At the end of the year, the National Battlefields Commission's cheque had arrived for $2500, which Langton invested early in 1925 in short-term debentures, ending the Society's financial problems until well after the period of this study (see Table 4).[170]

Rightly or wrongly, the exchange of letters over the illustrations and criticism by Ganong of the notes to Volume II shook the confidence of Wallace and Wrong in Biggar. As Wallace wrote to Wrong:

> I must confess that I have not great confidence in Mr. Biggar as an editor, and I think some of Professor Ganong's criticisms are only too well justified; but we have accepted Mr. Biggar as

---

163 Ibid., item 66, Minutes of Council, 2 May 1911.
164 Ibid., box 49, fol. 6, Biggar to Langton, 18 November 1924.
165 Ibid.
166 At this time the Society had little money in their Current Account, but it never had a deficit (Table 4).
167 Ibid., Langton to Biggar, 2 December 1924. Biggar had wanted the picture because Champlain had dedicated the *Quatriesme Voyage* to Henri de Bourbon, Prince de Condé.
168 Ibid., fol. 7, Biggar to Langton, 6 January 1925.
169 Ibid., fol. 4, Ganong to Langton, 7 January 1924.
170 Ibid., item 66, Minutes of Council, 17 December, 1924.

general editor and it seems to me we must leave details of this sort [the notes] in his hands. The only matter which I am concerned about is the question of the expense of additions and illustrations put in at the last moment.[171]

On a more conciliatory note, Biggar got permission to "go ahead with Condé" and an explanation of Cameron's delays: "There has been much excuse for poor Cameron, as his wife has been slowly dying for more than a year and all the time he could spare has been devoted to her."[172]

Early in March, Biggar wrote Langton that he had received Cameron's and Squair's corrected page proofs, accepted all but a few of their notes and returned them to Spottiswoode for a second set of proofs to be returned to Squair and Cameron for comment.[173] In the same letter he asked how Cameron was getting along with Volume III. In the knowledge that no book had been published in over a year and fearing new delays and additional typesetting, Langton wrote back that Biggar was not to send the new proofs to Squair and Cameron but to do the editing himself.[174] Even though Biggar agreed to this suggestion, he sent Squair and Cameron his Preface to the volume as well as the proofs explaining however that they were in final form adding "they can protest by cable if anything is wrong."[175] This was a mistake because Squair and Cameron complained not only to Wallace about Biggar's editing but also to Council. The two agreed however not to press objections in order, "to get on with it," but Biggar was told to make the changes proposed by Squair as long as the volume was not held up.[176] To Squair, Wallace wrote, "We have all suffered a little in this respect from Biggar's editing."[177] The inclusion of Squair's and Cameron's "changes" were however too late because Biggar had taken the final proofs to the printer and now wanted his £50 for editing Volume II.[178] In response Langton wrote a long letter explaining that Biggar was only getting £28 because he had already been paid $150; that Squair got $150 for the translation and Cameron $60 for collating the text. He then went on for several more pages explaining Squair's objections, Champlain Society editing procedures, English usage as adapted from Ballantyne's "The Style of the House" and ended with the comment that the translators are responsible for the final text and not the editor who should only point out ambiguities or inaccuracies.[179] Biggar was of course annoyed

---

171   Ibid., box 39, Wallace to Wrong, 16 January 1925.
172   Ibid., box 49, fol.7, Langton to Biggar, 9 February 1925. Elizabeth (Read) Cameron died 7 January. 1925. University of Toronto Archives, A1973–0026, Graduate Records, box 048, fol. "Cameron."
173   Ibid., Biggar to Langton, 4 March 1925.
174   Ibid., Wallace to Biggar, 16 March 1925.
175   Ibid., Biggar to Wallace, 1 April, 4 April and 19 April 1925.
176   Ibid., fol. 8, Wallace to Biggar, 21 April 1925. Item 65, Minutes of 7 May, 1925.
177   Ibid., Wallace to Squair, 22 May 1925.
178   Ibid., Biggar to Wallace, 13 May 1925.
179   Ibid., Langton to Biggar, 21 May 1925.

when he received only £28. In his response to Langton he pointed out that an agreement for payment of £50 made well before the War should be revised, but understood why it was not. On the other hand, he had been doing the notes that Squair had "refused" to do and went on his own expense to Morrison Island to prove that Champlain did not go to Allumette Island as others had thought. In other words, he felt he "deserved" a bonus. As for his editorial work, he had simply been doing what he did for Volume I,[180] that his English usage was set by Spottiswoode and that Council had no business chiding him for editing Squair's and Cameron's texts since Council had ordered him to make changes without consulting the two, besides "Squair's French is not as complete as he thinks."[181] Biggar concluded that these problems were the result of "rushing" the volume.

On 28 May, Spottiswoode wrote that the proofs were in hand and that they would print 550 copies and 1150 copies of the illustrations.[182] On August 29 the crates of books were shipped on the *Brecon* for distribution in September.[183] The final cost of Volume II was $3933.28 as computed from the ledger.[184] Of this total, the invoice from Spottiswoode came to $3044.09 (£627/3/9) of which about £46 was for "revisions."[185] The editorial fees had remained at $600. Hoping to avoid misunderstanding and the escalation of costs in future volumes Council passed a resolution that "all publications of the Society shall be submitted to Council in their final form and approved before being sent to the printer…and the order to begin printing shall emanate directly from Council."[186]

Biggar was disappointed in the volume and especially his remuneration. To receive only £28 was "very upsetting" but he would do his "best to stick to my bargain."[187] He was not, however, able to let the matter rest. Late in October he wrote to Langton, the treasurer, asking that Council grant him an extra £20 ($100) for Volume II. Referring to an earlier letter he had received from Langton, Biggar quoted "You say their [Council] liberality will largely depend upon my keeping down the cost of printing," well he had "tried that with Cameron and Ganong and spent weeks of extra time on the volume. Your letter did not exactly stimulate me when I have striven so hard in the past to attain this very object." He finished by saying he was selling his Canadian books to make ends meet, that "everyone was pleased" the extra documents were included and that he will

---

180   In this Biggar was correct. Walker settled the matter in 1916–17, to which Langton was witness.
181   Ibid., Biggar to Langton, 9 June 1925.
182   Ibid., Spottiswoode to Jarvis, 28 May 1925.
183   Ibid., fol. 9, Spottiswoode to Jarvis, 27 August 1925.
184   Ibid., item 15, General Ledger 1906–1962.
185   Ibid., fol. 9, Spottiswoode to Jarvis 22 October 1925; and Langton to Spottiswoode, 1 December 1925.
186   Ibid., Wallace to Biggar, 16 October 1925. Ibid., item 66, Minutes of Council, 13 October 1925.
187   Ibid., fol. 8, Biggar to Wallace, 31 July 1925.

try hard to finish the six volumes, but "will do Volume III in any event."[188] This letter drew another response from Langton, namely that there would be no bonus because they could not afford it. The members were now getting only one book for a fee of $10 instead of the two promised in 1905, and that the cost of the two Champlain volumes if projected to six volumes would cost nearly $30,000. "How can we afford now to vote you a bonus?" To make matters worse, Langton referred back to the original contract in which "you named the terms of your editorship – *viz* $500 per volume to include all the editorial work and translation…I don't think you should press now for any further additional payment."[189] Biggar had to reply to this letter both in order to correct errors and to review why in his opinion costs for the first two volumes had been so high. The editorial costs, he contended, were set by Wrong and the Council and that he had nothing to do with "fixing the original terms."[190] In fact he had at first refused the offer to edit the volumes but accepted when he was told it was not much more than the work he had done on the *Trading Companies of New France*.[191] What delayed Volume I? First, regarding the French editing: Roy had done nothing and then died; the business with Myrand "took months;" after Cultru started, he died, and then Cameron took over. In each case he had to start afresh, and all that for $350. For Volume II, Wrong never contemplated that he (Biggar) would have to do all the notes and extra work doing what Squair and Cameron were supposed to do in collating the French text.[192] He also thought he had done a service to the Society through his trip to Pembroke during the summer. Finally, the volume was "rushed through the press at great personal inconvenience," and all he got was $130 more that Squair! Now, he wrote, he had to sell his library to educate his children and is told that because of the costs incurred to the volumes, the Society could not vote him a bonus of $100.[193] There is no doubt that Biggar was in desperate financial shape and had hoped for a change in the terms to which he had agreed in 1910. Finally, on 18 January 1927, the Society voted him a $100 bonus for Volume II, too late to soothe the ill feelings that had developed, and he did not get a change in the terms.[194]

By 1925 everyone knew that rapid movement of the *Works* through the press, depended on the speed with which Cameron could collate the French texts. Further hold ups and added expenses could occur with last moment additions of extra

---

188 Ibid., fol. 9, Biggar to Langton, 22 October 1925.
189 Ibid., Langton to Biggar, 5 November 1925.
190 For Biggar's understanding of the final offer from Wrong see: Box 28a, fol. 3, Biggar to Wrong, 15 April 1911. Appendix VII.
191 Biggar, *The Early Trading Companies of New France*.
192 Biggar had done a great deal of the collating of the 1613 text while in London using an original in his possession.
193 Ibid., fol. 10, Biggar to Langton, 23 December 1925.
194 Ibid., item 15, General Ledger, 1906–1962.

documents and pictures. The expected publishing date 1924 was missed largely for these reasons (see Table 2 c). The question was what could be done about it? Council's insistence that additions to a volume had to be cleared by them was really "nickel and dime" management that could detract from a volume. More serious were repeated type setting of the text and trans-oceanic mailing of the galleys. The major factors however, that led to delays and extra type setting were Cameron's collation and corrections. Unfortunately, the Council and its executive never really understood the editing problems Cameron was facing; a complicated printing history that had led to seemingly endless variations in the printed texts and the scattered nature of the texts through North American and European libraries. All they saw was a super sensitive, seemingly overly fussy editor in Cameron who wanted to produce a definitive text and would not be rushed. By now Cameron was totally committed to produce a text that was in every way superior to that of Laverdière's *Œuvres* and little was going to deter him, but even he did not know that Champlain's texts and language were going to become much more difficult than what had already been collated, translated and published.

VOLUME III, 1926 TO 1930

The third volume of the series was to contain Champlain's third book *Voyages Et Descouvertures* first published in 1619 by Collet and republished by the same printer in 1620 and 1627, as well as the first and second books of the *Premier Partie* of *Les Voyages* printed simultaneously by three Paris printers, Collet, Le Mur and Sevestre in 1632. (For complete references to Champlain's books, see Appendix IV) Of these books, Langton had finished translating *Voyages Et Descouvertures* in September 1914, for which he was paid $135.[195] While Volume II was winding down, Langton sent Biggar his translation,[196] which Biggar began editing in January 1925.[197] A few weeks later he wrote to Ganong about translating the second part of Volume III and to Squair about translating Volume IV.[198] Ganong was the logical choice to translate the first two books of Part I of *Les Voyages, 1632*, because they were Champlain's summary of his early voyages to the St. Lawrence and Acadia which Ganong had already translated for Volume I. Similarly, Squair was the logical person to translate the material destined for Volume IV because most of it was a summary of the voyage to the St. Lawrence which he had translated for Volume II. Both however declined the offer.[199] It now fell to Biggar to translate the part destined for Volume III using Ganong's translation and notes from

---

195 Ibid., box 48, fol. 7, Biggar to Creighton, 6 September 1914; Ibid., item 15, General Ledger, 1906–1962, September 18, 1914.
196 Ibid., box 49, fol. 6, Langton to Biggar, 7 October 1924.
197 Ibid., fol. 5, Biggar to Wallace, 19 January 1925.
198 Ibid., Biggar to Wallace, 12 February 1925.
199 Squair was writing his memoirs, *The Autobiography of a Teacher of French* (Toronto, University of Toronto Press, 1928). The book was published just after he died the same year.

Volume I as a guide.²⁰⁰ In early March, Biggar submitted a list of illustrations for Volume III and as usual was wondering how Cameron was coming along with the French text.²⁰¹ Two weeks later he resubmitted his request for illustrations and stated that he was ready to go to the printer as soon as he received Cameron's text and permission to proceed from the Council. He also added that being "hard up" he hoped he would be granted £50 for his work on the volume.²⁰² Ten days later Biggar fired off another letter asking Wallace for Cameron's text since he thought Cameron had finished it.²⁰³ At the Council Meeting of 7 May, it was decided only to include the six original illustrations in Champlain's *Voyages Et Descouvertures* and the large 1632 map from *Les Voyages* but not the pictures of Louis XIII and Cardinal Richelieu requested by Biggar.²⁰⁴ In reply Biggar wrote that the two pictures would only add $10 to the cost of the volume and he wanted them because Champlain had dedicated his books to these two heads of state.²⁰⁵ Instead of getting his wish he was ordered to send Volume III to the printer no later than September 1926, for distribution to the membership by the end of that year.²⁰⁶

Realizing that nothing further could be done with Biggar and that everything hinged on Cameron, the executive now turned to him to complete the French collation because, "Biggar wants to go to press."²⁰⁷ Cameron replied that he had the collation done but not yet the notes, that he had a heavy exam schedule, was "very tired" and had many other pressing things to do.²⁰⁸

Cameron was now given a brief respite while Langton dealt with the printing costs of Champlain's large *Carte de la nouvelle france…1632*. Because of its size this map had to be printed on a sheet of paper 96.5 cm by 61 cm (3'2" by 2'). In July the Society received an estimate from Spottiswoode that 1200 copies of the map would cost £40/10/-, or 550 copies for £26/10/- with an offer to reprint the extra 650 copies for the "popular edition" for £17/10/- at a later date. In order to keep expenses down, Langton decided to take the offer to print 550 copies but informed Spottiswoode that he was not abandoning plans to do the popular edition. A few weeks later however, the Society ordered the full 1200 copies.²⁰⁹

Having dealt with the map, Wallace and Langton now returned to their attempts to prod Cameron. Fearing delays, Wallace gave advice to Biggar on handling Cameron:

---

200 Ibid., fol. 14, Langton to Biggar, 13 January 1926.
201 Ibid., fol. 7, Biggar to Langton, 4 March 1925.
202 Ibid., fol. 14, Biggar to Langton, 18 March 1925.
203 Ibid., fol. 7, Biggar to Wallace, 26 March 1925.
204 Ibid., item 66, Minutes of Council, 7 May 1925.
205 Ibid., box 49, fol. 8, Biggar to Langton, 9 June 1925.
206 Ibid., Langton to Biggar, 23 June 1925.
207 Ibid., fol. 14, Langton to Cameron, 22 May 1925.
208 Ibid., Cameron to Langton, 2 June 1925.
209 Ibid., Spottiswoode to Langton, 18 July and 1 September 1925. Langton to Biggar, 21 August 1925, and Langton to Spottiswoode, 21 August 1925. Wallace to Spottiswoode, 16 September 1925.

Don't abridge anything, he counts the letters; don't make changes because of the delays getting them to him and back; he was most upset that you changed the words "French text" to "French texts" in his introductory note to Volume III—I have to sit here and listen to all this, so please, for heaven's sake, do not change anything that will pass muster…Personally I am not concerned very much about what the volume looks like so long as we get it out.[210]

Having earlier rejected pictures of Louis XIII and Richelieu, Wallace now told Biggar to add pictures of the title pages of the 1619 and 1632 volumes.

In February 1926, the battle to get a French text from Cameron began in earnest. Langton wrote demanding the text, to which Cameron replied that he was waiting for a "few photostats" from Ottawa.[211] In May Wallace wrote to Biggar that they were still waiting for Cameron, "I have never known anything quite like him."[212] A week later a letter arrived from Cameron explaining that he had a "heavy exam schedule;" that the Ottawa photostats were not "quite as wanted," and that he will be "on leave" next year to check out the Paris archives.[213] Seeing the volume slip into the following year, Langton demanded that he wanted to have the "text now," before Cameron left for Europe, and that corrections could be done on the galley proofs.[214] In September Cameron let Langton know that he would have the text "next week" and that Champlain's syntax was never worse than in the 1619–1620 text.[215] By mid October nothing further had been heard from Cameron.[216]

Late in January 1927, Biggar was wondering who was going to pay £2/9/- for typing the text of the first part of *Les Voyages, 1632* that he had translated for Volume III, and the whereabouts of Cameron's collation.[217] The answers were as expected; Biggar was responsible for the typing fee out of the stipend he got for translating the text and that nothing had been heard from Cameron.[218] After a further series of letters to Cameron, Wallace finally managed to report to Biggar that he had obtained Cameron's text and forwarded it to him. The delay had been due to "difficult problems with the various editions of the 1619 text" and that Cameron wanted to add a note to Volume III regarding bibliographical information on the text.[219] On 11 April, Biggar wrote back to

---

210 Ibid., Wallace to Biggar, 11 September 1925.
211 Ibid., fol. 15, Langton to Cameron. 16 February and Cameron to Langton, 18 February 1926.
212 Ibid., Wallace to Biggar, 21 May 1926.
213 Ibid., Cameron to Wallace, 27 May 1926. Cameron went on "retirement leave" in 1926–27 and retired from the university in 1927. In his retirement he decided to go to Europe to continue his search for variant texts of *Voyages Et Descouvertures* and *Les Voyages, 1632*, the very texts that Langton was hoping were already finished.
214 Ibid., Langton to Cameron, 2 June 1926.
215 Ibid., fol. 16, Cameron to Langton, no date [late September 1926].
216 Ibid., Biggar to Wallace, 14 October 1926.
217 Ibid., Biggar to Wallace, 27 January 1927.
218 Ibid., Langton to Biggar, 10 February 1927.
219 Ibid., Wallace to Cameron, 11 February; Biggar to Langton, 2 March; Wallace to Cameron, 17 March; Wallace to Biggar 25 March 1927. Champlain, *The Works,* ed. Biggar, volume III (1929): xi–xii.

Wallace that he had received Cameron's work on the first part of Volume III containing *Voyages Et Descouvertures*, but not the second part, containing the opening chapters of *Les Voyages, 1632*.[220] Wallace insisted however, that they had been in the parcel he had sent on 16 March, to which Biggar replied again that they were not among the papers he received.[221] Wallace eventually solved the mystery of Cameron's "lost" French text. Cameron had delivered both texts to him but when Wallace turned his back Cameron had removed the text of *Les Voyages* from the parcel and surreptitiously taken it home without Wallace's knowledge in order to do more work on it. It took Wallace over a week to get the text back.[222] In the same letter Wallace informed Biggar that for reasons of cost the Society was thinking of ending their printing arrangements with Spottiswoode in favour of the University of Toronto Press. After an exchange of letters with Spottiswoode, the Society decided to move the regular series to Toronto, but finish Champlain with Biggar and Spottiswoode in London.[223]

Sometime in the summer of 1927 Cameron retired from the university and departed for Europe to devote himself fully to collating the remaining Champlain volumes. Writing to Wallace from Menton, France,[224] on 14 February 1928, he explained that he had been to Edinburgh, London and Paris collating the 1619, 1620 and 1627 texts that are in the Bibliothèque nationale, and Bibliothèque de l'Arsenal in Paris; that he also collated some of the 1632 texts and found others in the Bibliothèque Sainte-Geneviève, Paris; that he tried to visit Biggar in London but was told he was in Canada and that Biggar "was in a very broken down condition." While in London he retrieved the text for Volume III from Biggar's secretary, changed a number of notes according to his research in Paris, and saw Champlain's 1632 map being printed.[225] Two weeks later Wallace wrote back thanking Cameron for the news that the map was being run off, "which must have been done at Biggar's request who is in the habit of sending things to them without consulting us."[226] Although he should have known better, Wallace informed Cameron that in view of the production schedule of Wood's *The Canadian War of 1812*, Volume III, part 2 (i.e. Wood's Volume IV), the Champlain volume would be held up and that he would have "ample time to make changes to Champlain III."[227]

By mid June, Biggar had not yet received the complete text for Volume III, which prompted an irritable note to Wallace: "What has happened to the manuscript for

---

220 Ibid., Biggar to Wallace, 11 April 1927.
221 Ibid. Wallace to Biggar, 21 April, and Biggar to Wallace 3 May 1927.
222 Ibid., fol. 17, Wallace to Biggar, 23 May 1927. In her "Speech, Part 2," p. 11, Julia Jarvis gives a delightful account of this incident but used considerable license in telling it.
223 Ibid., fol. 19, Spottiswoode to Wallace, 23 May, Wallace to Spottiswoode 6 June, Wallace to Spottiswoode, 4 July 1928. Item 67, Minutes of Council, 13 November 1928.
224 Menton is east of Monaco near the Italian border.
225 Ibid., fol. 19, Cameron to Wallace ("and only to Langton"), 14 February 1928.
226 The reader may recall that Wallace approved the price and printing of the map on 16 September 1925.
227 Ibid., Wallace to Cameron, 29 February 1928.

Champlain III please? Does the Society intend to proceed with its publication? Where will it be printed?"[228] A month later Volume III went to Spottiswoode and Biggar was informed that he would be sent the galleys and was urged to get the cost estimates for the eight pictures.[229] These came to £22/11/- for 550 copies and £3/6/- for 600 more providing they were printed at the same time. Council approved the printing of 1150 pictures on November 13, 1928, the same day that Henry Percival Biggar resigned from The Champlain Society requesting that his membership # 327 be assigned to the Institute of Historical Research in London.[230]

By the end of November 1928, the page proofs for Champlain III were finally ready and sent by Spottiswoode to Wallace.[231] From there they went to Cameron for proofreading and to add a few notes with the request that he was to send them to Biggar by mid February 1929.[232] A month later Biggar had not yet received the page proofs from Cameron, prompting Wallace to remind Cameron that Biggar must have the volume "ready by summer."[233] In mid April Biggar received some proofs from Wallace and two incomplete sets from Cameron, which left him wondering which ones he was supposed to use and when he would get the rest.[234] Cameron, however, had not yet completed revising the French text and notes. On July 16, he wrote Wallace that he had found that "certain copies" of *Les Voyages Et Descouvertures, 1627* contained the "oldest and uncorrected text" of the three printings, and that he would hurry to rewrite his notes.[235] A week later he complained to Wallace of the inaccurate translation of Volume III, that it was in fact "a mess" like Volume I and Lescarbot, which he must rework.[236] With what must have been a sinking feeling, all Wallace could hope for was that this would not delay the volume because that would be "a serious matter" for Society finances.[237] In early September, Biggar had received Cameron's revisions, "corrected" them, and returned them to Cameron. At the end of September however, Cameron had still not returned the proofs to Biggar.[238] A month later, Cameron informed Wallace that he was now trying to finish his second revisions of the first half of Volume III and another month later wrote again complaining loudly of Biggar's

---

228 Ibid., fol. 17, Biggar to Wallace, 20 June 1928.
229 Ibid., fol. 18, Wallace to Biggar, 20 July 1928.
230 Ibid., Item 67, Minutes of Council, 13 November 1928. Biggar found the membership fees too expensive and felt discouraged by the treatment he was receiving from the Society.
231 Ibid., fol. 18, Spottiswoode to Wallace, 30 November 1928.
232 Ibid., Wallace to Cameron, 11 February and Wallace to Biggar, 21 February 1929.
233 Ibid., fol. 19, Wallace to Cameron, 14 March 1929.
234 Ibid., Wallace to Biggar, March 23, Biggar to Wallace, 10 April and Biggar to Wallace, 3 July 1929.
235 Ibid., Cameron to Wallace, 16 July 1929.
236 Ibid., fol. 20, Cameron to Wallace, 24 July 1929.
237 Ibid., Wallace to Cameron, 27 August 1929. The bank balance in 1929 was very low at $663 but the investment account had a balance of $8329 (see Table 4).
238 Ibid., Cameron to Wallace, 2 September and Wallace to Cameron, 30 September 1929.

editing; that, in fact, he would give up his remuneration if the Society would publish his "full account of the remarkable variations in the [1619, 1620 and 1627] texts."[239] Biggar in turn complained of the minutiae of Cameron's "corrections."[240] Wallace was furious that a feud between Biggar and Cameron was holding up the volume and had to take measures. To Cameron he wrote that he sympathized with him over the "unnecessary alterations in your notes," and to Biggar that he was to print Cameron's notes without changes and to cite costs in refusing to make more changes if Cameron submitted any at a later date.[241] On 23 November, Council sent Cameron and Biggar the same letter stating that:

> Mr. Biggar be instructed to proceed immediately with the printing of Champlain III; that he must use his own discretion with regard to the points at issue between Professor Cameron and himself; that in them he has final authority, but that he should be as generous as he can in acceding to the suggestions that Professor Cameron has made.[242]

Wallace received Cameron's final edited version in late November and sent it directly to the press. There the Spottiswoode "corrector" went over the marked-up proofs with Biggar, who was present to clear up any questions.[243]

Spottiswoode scheduled the volume to be sent to the membership by late February 1930.[244] In the meantime, Wallace and Biggar had to figure out how much each participant in the confusing production of the volume was to be paid. Cameron wanted $120 instead of the usual collating fee of $60 since he had done so much extra work on the volume. This drew the response from Biggar that, instead, Cameron should donate his fee toward the cost of all the corrections he caused. In the end Cameron received $100,[245] but deserved much more in view of spending his leave at his own expense unravelling the complicated history of Champlain's books and collating the variant texts. Langton received $120 even though he had already been paid $135 in September 1914 after he had finished his original translation.[246] Biggar was paid $280 and on 2 April, a bonus of $150 for completing Volume III and because he was editing

---

239   Ibid., Cameron to Wallace, 6 November 1929.
240   Ibid., fol. 41, Biggar to Wallace, 6 November 1929.
241   Ibid., fol. 20, Wallace to Cameron, 7 November and Wallace to Biggar, 18 November 1929.
242   Ibid. Wallace to Cameron and Wallace to Biggar, 23 November 1929. Also: item 67, Minutes of Council, 22 November 1929.
243   Ibid. Biggar to Wallace, 18 December 1929.
244   Ibid. fol. 21, Spottiswoode to Jarvis, 7 February 1930. Although Volume III bears a printer's date of 1929, it in fact was not printed until early in 1930.
245   Ibid. fol. 22, Biggar to Wallace, 5 March and Wallace to Biggar 18 March 1930.
246   Ibid. Wallace to Biggar, 18 March 1930. The extra money was eventually repaid.

Champlain on a "pre-war Contract."[247] The final bill from Spottiswoode was $2705.14, bringing the total for Volume III to $3490.14.[248]

On April 17, 1930, at the Annual Meeting of the Society, Cameron's work was recognized by the statement that he had examined many copies of Champlain's works found in Canada, the United States, England and France, and that:

> ...in some cases found extraordinary differences even in copies of the same edition; differences which show the influence at work of Champlain's text even while it was going through the printer's hands. In this respect Professor Cameron's collation will be found a distinct advance upon the hitherto authoritative text of Champlain published by Abbé Laverdière.[249]

There is absolutely no doubt that Cameron's leave, retirement and his trip in 1927–28 to collate copies of Champlain's books in European libraries, added immeasurably to the project and undoubtedly shortened the time it took the last three volumes to appear in print. A few weeks before his death on 30 September 1944, he donated his huge collection of notes, photographs of Champlain documents and some original Champlain volumes to the University of Toronto Library.[250] It appears that he published nothing on this material except the notes found in the six Champlain volumes.

VOLUME IV, 1930 TO 1932

The fourth volume was to contain the *Premier Partie* to the end of the *Livre Quatriesme* of *Les Voyages, 1632*, the period from 1608 to the beginning of 1620. John Squair, who had translated the text for Volume II, declined in 1925 to translate the text for Volume IV, but Wallace managed to persuade Langton to undertake Volume IV just as Volume III was going to press. In his letter to Biggar he wondered if he should offer Langton $50 or $100,[251] to which Biggar replied that $75 should be sufficient.[252] By September, Langton was finding errors in the Laverdière text he was translating, which had not yet been collated by Cameron. To his chagrin he was finding even more errors in

---

247 Ibid. fol. 21, Wallace to Biggar, 2 April 1930. Item 67, Minutes of Council, 1 April 1930.
248 Ibid. item 15, General Ledger, 1906–1962.
249 Ibid., item 67, Minutes of Council, Minutes of Annual Meeting, 17 April 1930.
250 University of Toronto Archives, A1973-0026, Graduate Records, box 048, fol. "Cameron." On his 1927–28 trip to Europe Cameron travelled with a camera and took hundreds of photographs of the Champlain texts in the libraries he visited, as well as ordering photostats from libraries that had the facilities to produce them. Some of his editing and photographs are in the Thomas Fisher Library but are not catalogued under Cameron's name. See for example part of *Les Voyages, 1632* from Volume VI of Laverdière's *Œuvres*, marked up by Cameron in: MS Coll. 50, Box 65. Most of Cameron's photographs and photostats are catalogued in Fisher under: Champlain, Samuel de, 1567–1635. Local call numbers: G10-0035; E10-0450; G10-00033; G10-00034; E10-0456; E10-00450 and E10-6450, seem to pertain to *Les Voyages, 1632*. Other call numbers in this series refer to photographs and editorial notes on Champlain's other books.
251 Ibid., fol. 22, Wallace to Biggar, 8 February 1930.
252 Ibid., Biggar to Wallace, 26 February 1930.

Squair's translation of the more detailed version of this material already published by the Society in Volume II.[253]

Early in the new year (1931), frustrations with Cameron began to surface again. The procedure that had been worked out was that Langton was to translate from the imperfect Laverdière French text and send his work to Cameron who would make corrections to Langton's translation using the collated French text he was still working on. The problem with this was that the ever-cautious Cameron now felt responsible for both the French and the English texts "…examining the most minute details of the text as if it were the Holy Scriptures, and his salvation depended on it."[254] By mid March, enough pressure had been brought on Cameron that Wallace could send what he thought was the final manuscript of Champlain IV to Biggar for editorial changes. He also informed Spottiswoode that the firm would soon receive the manuscript from Biggar and were to produce four galley proofs, one to be returned to Biggar and three to Wallace.[255] A wary Biggar responded that he was "not going to touch Cameron's notes;" that he was in a nursing home because of ill health but would nevertheless try to work on the volume.[256]

On April eighth, part of the manuscript went from Biggar to Spottiswoode, followed on 20 May by the rest.[257] Spottiswoode set the type and sent the proofs of the French text and Langton's English translation to Cameron, Biggar and Langton on 4 June.[258] Once the proofs were in hand, an extraordinary exchange of letters began between Biggar, Wallace, Langton and Cameron, that lasted from July 1931 to the end of January 1932, containing not only a massive number of changes to the translation but increasingly insulting comments about each others competence.[259] At the root of the problem was that Cameron had been far from completing his collation of the extremely complex variations in the 1632 texts that he was examining when Wallace insisted on having the manuscript rendered into galley proofs. By mid December Cameron was still finding new variants of the text in Canada,[260] and on 19 January 1932, when Council ordered the volume go to press,[261] he claimed that he had collated "only" eleven copies of the 1632 text and three of the 1640 reprint and felt he should be examining more.[262] A second, equally serious problem had occurred when Wallace asked Cameron to correct Langton's translation while he was collating the French text. Cameron did extensive

---

253   Ibid., fol. 23, Langton to Biggar, 23 September 1930.
254   Ibid., Wallace to Biggar, 4 March 1931.
255   Ibid., Wallace to Biggar, 10 March and Wallace to Hanson (Spottiswoode), 10 March 1931.
256   Ibid., Biggar to Wallace, 23 March 1931.
257   Ibid., fol. 24, Biggar to Langton, 8 April and Biggar to Wallace 20 May 1931.
258   Ibid., Spottiswoode to Wallace, 4 June 1931.
259   Most of the thirty to forty letters are contained in Box 49, fol. 25 to the end of fol. 28.
260   Ibid., fol. 27, Biggar to Wallace, 16 December 1931.
261   Ibid., fol. 28, Wallace to Biggar, 19 January 1932.
262   See Cameron's introductory notes in Volumes III (1929), IV (1932) and V (1933) of *The Works*.

"corrections" but did not check these with Langton before he returned the texts to Biggar, an oversight for which Cameron later apologized.²⁶³ Biggar of course, made further "corrections" annoying both Langton and Cameron. Wallace was not sympathetic to Cameron's "endless corrections" and took the matter to the Council of the Society who ordered Cameron to turn his texts over to Biggar and henceforth work with Langton to speed up the collation of Champlain V and VI."²⁶⁴ The same day Cameron received the letter regarding the Council's decision he responded to Wallace:

> You say you cannot see that I need bother myself with the corrections of the translation at all. That depends on how much you care whether our translation is good or bad. You have on several occasions said that you are not interested in that, so long as our volumes come out at the time fixed for them! I have allowed you to have your way more than once, notably in the issue of Vol. III. And what is the result? An English translation that is open to a great deal of criticism, and scarcely a credit to the Champlain Society.

To emphasize his point that he was doing an excellent job cleaning up Langton's English translation, Cameron quoted from a letter that Biggar had sent to him:

> 'Your [Cameron's] new translations are excellent and show a masterful insight into the language upon which I congratulate you very heartily. You seem to me to have solved a number of very difficult problems. I have no doubt Langton will be as pleased as I am with your renderings'…[From this Cameron concluded] As for any collaboration in the collation of the text [with Langton]—the less that is mentioned the better.²⁶⁵

The pinnacle of silliness was reached over the translation of the French word *branée*, which Biggar had rendered as "bran-mash," a translation Langton described as "nonsense," accusing Biggar of having invented it. Langton insisted that the word should be "swill or hog-wash."²⁶⁶ Biggar wrote back, "You flatter me about [inventing] bran-mash! You'll find it in volume III, page 129, Cameron wanted it again…but let us use hog-wash if the dictionary gives it." ²⁶⁷ In the printed text the word "swill" was used.²⁶⁸

Wallace finally ended the orgy of corrections by ordering Biggar not to wait for Cameron: "He will go on making changes until the crack of doom," and that Council had authorized him to print the text.²⁶⁹ To make the matter absolutely clear, Langton also wrote to Biggar, not to wait for Cameron's "second and third thoughts," and not to send him the revised proofs, "the passage backwards and forwards of revised and

---

263   Ibid., box 49, fol. 24, Biggar to Wallace, 15 April and Cameron to Langton, 1 July 1931.
264   Ibid., item 67, Minute Book, 1924–1948, Minutes of Council 23 October 1931.
265   Ibid., box 37, fol. 48, Cameron to Wallace, 23 October 1931.
266   Ibid., box 49, fol. 27, Langton to Biggar, 17 December 1931.
267   Ibid., fol. 28, Biggar to Langton, 11 January 1932.
268   See p. 308 in Volume IV of the Biggar edition.
269   Ibid., fol. 28, Wallace to Biggar, 19 January 1932.

re-revised proofs should cease."²⁷⁰ On 12 February, Council reported that all proofs were now with Biggar and that "no more proofs were to be sent out."²⁷¹ Three weeks later Biggar received a cable from Cameron with more changes and the news that still more were to come!²⁷² To no avail, the book was being printed and to be ready by 30 April, whereupon Cameron threatened not to collate Volume V and VI.²⁷³ Although Biggar was getting letters from Cameron, it was really Wallace who bore the brunt of Cameron's attack. Commiserating with Biggar, Wallace wrote that: "Cameron is writing endless letters to Tyrrell,²⁷⁴ Langton and me," he is "mortally offended" that Langton will be collaborating with him on the remaining volumes and was told that there was no need for collaboration if he got the texts in on time.²⁷⁵ As president of The Champlain Society, the gentlemanly Tyrrell thought he could solve the problems between Cameron and Biggar if "we talk informally and endeavour to come to some pleasant and satisfactory arrangement," but Wallace advised him against it because "Biggar is editor in chief and Council should not come between them…if Cameron does not like his decisions then he can resign." ²⁷⁶ Early in May Wallace could report to Biggar that Cameron was working on Champlain V, but: "…if he had resigned I do not think it would have been an unmitigated disaster."²⁷⁷

On 20 April 1932 Champlain IV rolled off the press and was shipped to Canada on the *Beaverford* by Spottiswoode on April 28.²⁷⁸ As for remuneration, Biggar had eventually persuaded Wallace that Langton should get $175 in view of all the extra work and not $75 as had previously been agreed to.²⁷⁹ Council however noticed finally that they had paid him $120 too much for Volume III, which he agreed to pay back.²⁸⁰ According to the Society's Ledger, Cameron received a total of $180 and Biggar $250 as well as a bonus of $150 and repayment of incidental fees of $31.52. The printing costs from Spottiswoode were $1916.70, making the total cost of Volume IV $2703.22²⁸¹ Finally, production costs of the *Works* were almost in line with the other Champlain Society volumes (see Table 3 a).

---

270 Ibid., fol. 28, Langton to Biggar, 28 January 1932.
271 Ibid., item 67, Minute Book, 1924–1948, Minutes of Council 12 February 1932. Also: box 49, fol. 28, Wallace to Biggar, 13 February 1932.
272 Ibid., fol. 28, Biggar to Wallace, 2 March 1932.
273 Ibid., fol. 28, Biggar to Wallace, 16 March 1932.
274 Joseph Burr Tyrrell was President of the Champlain Society from 1927–1932.
275 Ibid., fol. 28, Wallace to Biggar, 30 March 1932.
276 Ibid., box 38, Tyrrell to Wallace, 29 January, and Wallace to Tyrrell, 30 January 1937.
277 Ibid., box 49, fol. 29, Wallace to Biggar, 4 May 1932.
278 Ibid., fol. 28, Biggar to Wallace 20 April, and fol. 29, Spottiswoode to Jarvis, 29 April 1932.
279 Ibid., fol. 25, Biggar to Wallace, 7 October 1931.
280 Ibid., fol. 29, Langton to Biggar, 18 June 1932.
281 Ibid., item 15, General Ledger, 1906–1962.

Volumes V and VI, 1932 to 1936

With the *Seconde Partie* of *Les Voyages, 1632*, to be published as Volumes V and VI, the Society was treading on new ground because none of this material had previously been translated into English. Volumes V and VI, except for the *Traitté de la Marine*, had been assigned for translation to the respected French Canadian scholar and critic William Dawson LeSueur as early as 1909. LeSueur had finished his work for Volume V in December 1910 for which he was paid $100.[282] His translation for Volume VI was apparently finished in September 1914.[283] LeSueur died in 1917, never to see any of his work appear in print.[284] Langton agreed to translate the *Traitté* in 1931, completing it a year later, with the comment that "...a more incoherent and ungrammatical piece of French could hardly exist in print."[285]

Cameron was of course responsible for collating the French text for both volumes and decided to go to Quebec City for the summer of 1932 to check through more original editions. Early in the summer he wrote optimistically, "If things go as I expect, the next volume of our Champlain can be issued early next year."[286] After six weeks of work he had managed to collate ten more texts of the 1632 and 1640 printings, of which he took over 600 photographs. Things, however did not go as expected. Like Langton with the *Traitté*, Cameron found Champlain's French in the *Seconde Partie* of *Les Voyages, 1632*, "difficult" and "some passages were hopelessly confused."[287] Early November Wallace reported to Biggar that Cameron had just about finished collating Champlain V and that he wanted to see LeSueur's translation, but, fearing the usual delays, Biggar was not to give it to him since the book had to go to the members by spring.[288] Instead, Wallace thought Biggar could check the translation himself once he had Cameron's collated text. On November 11, Wallace finished sending various parts of Cameron's text to Biggar and suggested that Cameron be shown the galley proofs only when they were finished. Apparently Cameron had told him they could be corrected quickly depending on "the attitude of the General Editor [Biggar]."[289] Even at this late date Biggar still complained that Cameron wanted to "reach the *texte primitif*," but that he felt some consideration should be given to the French reader, by "correcting

---

282 Ibid., item 6, Letterbook, August 1910 to November 1911. Walker to Wrong, 22 December 1910. Item 15, General Ledger, 1906–1962, payment 30 December 1910.
283 Ibid., box 48, fol. 7, Biggar to Creighton, 6 September 1914.
284 Upon being notified that LeSueur had died, The Champlain Society purchased his twelve Champlain volumes from his daughter Miss Beatrice LeSueur for $70. Ibid., box 36, fol. 46, 15 October 1917.
285 Ibid., box 49, fol. 25, Biggar to Wallace, 19 August, and Wallace to Biggar, 31 August 1931. Ibid., fol. 30, Langton to Biggar, 15 August 1932.
286 Ibid., box 37, fol. 49, Cameron to Wallace, 18 June 1932.
287 Ibid., Cameron to Wallace, 25 September 1932.
288 Ibid., box 49, fol. 30, Wallace to Biggar, 5 November 1932.
289 Ibid., Wallace to Biggar, 9 and 11 November 1932.

the text" and "giving the faulty reading in a note" rather than *vice versa*.[290] In spite of Wallace's instructions to the contrary, by the end of November Biggar had sent parts of LeSueur's translation to Cameron and promised he would send the rest later, because "his changes are often great improvements."[291] Wallace's reaction was predictable. He was "sorry" Biggar had done so and now expected a "serious delay."[292]

In mid March 1933, Biggar reported that Cameron had been "a great help" with the translation and that Volume V was now with the printer,[293] to which Wallace responded that he was glad that Biggar and Cameron were getting along better.[294] As the proofs were being produced, Biggar sent Wallace a request to include a map, "the only illustration in the volume." William Ganong had sent him a portion from an Admiralty Chart of a section of the St. Lawrence River that he felt should accompany Champlain's detailed description of the river between Saguenay and Québec. The cost of including this map would be £4/7/6, of which Wallace approved.[295]

The book went to the press on 17 May, the quickest production of any Champlain book, but Wallace had hoped it would be in print by 10 May and blamed Biggar for letting Cameron see the proofs.[296] In view of this delay, Wallace now explained to Biggar and the press, that since Volume V would not reach Canada before June 5, Spottiswoode should hold delivery to the beginning of September. Wallace's argument was that it would be "useless" to try delivery of the books when people are on holidays at their "summerhouses."[297] Biggar was, of course, disappointed to hear that distribution of the volume was going to be delayed, "after working so hard to make it accurate." He thought Wallace's argument bizarre and suggested that the books could still be delivered because people do not go on holidays until "after the schools close at the end of July."[298] Cameron however, thought that Champlain V "gained a very great deal" through the delay because it permitted the creation of a better text.[299] The book came off the press on 16 June but Wallace was adamant that it not be distributed in Canada until September since the Society had tried that once before which caused "endless

---

290 Ibid., Biggar to Wallace, 23 November 1932.
291 Ibid., Biggar to Wallace, 30 November 1932.
292 Ibid., Wallace to Biggar, 12 December 1932.
293 Ibid., fol. 31, Biggar to Wallace, 16 March 1933.
294 Ibid., Wallace to Biggar, 10 April 1933.
295 Ibid., Biggar to Wallace, 3 May, and Wallace to Biggar, 15 May 1933. Unfortunately this chart is not properly identified in Volume V (facing p. 178).
296 Ibid., Wallace to Biggar, 15 May, and Biggar to Wallace 17 May 1933.
297 Ibid., fol. 32, Wallace to Biggar, 22 May, and Wallace to Spottiswoode, 22 May 1933.
298 Ibid., Biggar to Wallace, 7 June 1933.
299 Ibid., box 37, fol. 50, Cameron to Wallace, 6 June 1932.

problems;" however, they could distribute it in England.[300] Spottiswoode shipped the books on the *Ausonia* on 4 August. They arrived in Toronto on 12 August.[301]

The production costs of Volume V were as follows: Biggar was paid $290 and a bonus of $150; Cameron got $60; LeSueur had been paid $100 on 30 December 1910, and Spottiswoode was paid $1988.29 for printing and shipping, for a grand total of $2588.29.[302] In a fit of generosity, Biggar suggested to Wallace that Cameron deserved more money for his revisions of LeSueur's translation and offered to give him half his bonus.[303] Wallace's response was that if Biggar wanted to give Cameron half, it was entirely up to him, not The Champlain Society.[304]

Biggar had begun work on Volume VI during mid–May 1933, and requested that Langton ask Cameron to look at the *Traitté* before it was sent to him, because "he gets Champlain's meanings rather well." In his opinion the LeSueur translation of Volume VI was "very good".[305] Biggar also raised the necessity of producing an index for the six volumes which, Wallace suggested, might be done by Julia Jarvis.[306]

Early in January 1934, Cameron received Langton's text but was not able to send the complete text for Volume VI to Biggar until December.[307] Judging from Cameron's notes, scribbled on the margins of Laverdière's version of the *Traitté*, this was a particularly difficult piece for Cameron to collate and Langton, with Cameron's help, to translate[308] (Figures 13, 14, 15, and 16). Cameron tried to make Wallace understand that collation and translation could, in Champlain's case, not be rushed:

> The punctuation and the [original] proofreading are deplorable in the last half of the 1632 volume. LeSueur has done remarkable work in squeezing the meaning out of it; but he doesn't get nearly everything quite right—Ora pro nobis.[309]

Because the original French of the *Traitté* was so mangled, it made interpretation of the mathematical parts of the text very difficult. For this reason Andrew Thomson of the Dominion Observatory in Ottawa, checked the *Traitté*'s mathematical statements.

---

300 Ibid., box 49, fol. 32, Biggar to Wallace, 16 June, and Wallace to Biggar 19 June 1933.
301 Ibid., Spottiswoode to Jarvis, 4 August, and Customs to Jarvis, 19 August 1933.
302 Ibid., Langton to Biggar, 17 August 1933. This letter mentions a payment to the Estate of W.D. LeSueur of $150, but this was probably the payment for Volume VI, since LeSueur was paid $100 for V in 1910. Ibid. General Ledger, 1906–1962.
303 Ibid., Biggar to Wallace, 26 August 1933.
304 Ibid., Wallace to Biggar, 25 September 1933.
305 Ibid., fol. 31, Biggar to Wallace, 17 May, and fol. 32, Biggar to Langton, 19 May 1933.
306 Ibid., fol. 32, Wallace to Biggar, 30 May, and Biggar to Wallace, 12 June 1933.
307 Ibid., box 37, fol. 50. Langton to Cameron, 13 January, Wallace to Cameron, 13 December 1934.
308 Ibid., box 65, Fol. 1–25
309 Ibid., box 37, fol. 50, Cameron to Wallace 12 December 1934. Ora pro nobis [Pray for us].

| 36 | TRAITTÉ DE LA |

Comme l'on doit dresser la table des estimes de iour en iour au papier iournal.

AV dessus est le long de la premiere colomne, & le long d'icelle escriuerez le mois, le iour & l'heure, que sortira le vaisseau du port ou autre endroit, au premier quarré sont les heures de deux en deux iusques à douze, & recommencer deux iusques à autre douze qui feront 24. heures, d'vn midy à autre, qu'assemblerez les lieuës de vostre estime, & pointer vostre carte pour sçauoir le lieu où sera le vaisseau, au deuxiesme est le rumb de vent sur lequel l'on nauige. Le troisiesme sont les lieuës du chemin de l'estime. Au quatriesme le rumb de vent qui fait cingler le vaisseau. Au cinquiesme, la hauteur où se treuuera le vaisseau : or notez que si partez à quatre heures du matin ou du soir, commencez à côter les lieuës de chemin. Au deuxiesme quarré où est marqué 4. heures, d'autant que de 4. à 6. il y a deux heures, afin de rencontrer le midy ou la minuict, pour se treuuer en l'ordre de douze heures, pour venir à 24. où finira l'estime. Ne faut oublier d'estre soigneux à toutes les fois que l'on peut, de prendre la hauteur & pointer la carte d'vn midy à l'autre d'autant que l'on ne sçauroit estre trop exact & diligent.

Comme si ie sortois du port par les 49. degrés de latitude, à quatre heures du matin, ie recognois que nauigeant à Ouest vn quart au Norrouest, estimant faire deux lieuës par heure, i'escrits deux lieuës en la colomne deuxiesme, & allant estimans iusqu'à douze

Figure 13. Samuel de Champlain, *Traitté de La Marine*, in: *Les Voyages de la nouvelle France...* (Paris: Louis Sevestre, 1632): 36. Compare with Figures 15 and 16.

NAVIGATION. 37

lieuës lefquelles venuës ie prens la hauteur s'il m'eft poſsible, la prenant ie treuue 48. degrés & 50. minutes, que ie mets à la fixiefme colomne vis à vis de 12. heures, aſſemblant le chemin de l'eſtime que i'ay fait depuis 4. heures du matin iufqu'à midy, ie treuue qu'il y a 9. heures qu'il faut doubler & font 18. lieuës de chemin, que marquerez fur la carte. Arreſtez le poinct iufqu'au lendemain que ferez le femblable, chofe facile fi l'on defire s'en feruir, car ie n'ay point veu que fort peu d'eſtimes qui ne foient en quelque confufion au papier iournal des rencontres, meſlant l'vn auec l'autre, ce qui donne de la peine & plus de foing, qu'il faut éuiter en cela le plus qu'il eſt pofsible, en mettant le tout par ordre, comme il fuit cy deſſous en ceſte table, qui n'eſt que pour 24. heures,

	Heures	Rumb pour la route.	Lieuës	Rumb pour le vent.	Degrés
Le 10. de May fortiſmes du Haure à 4. heures du matin.	2				
	4	A Oueſt $\frac{1}{4}$ au Norroueſt.	2	Le vent Nort.	49. de.
	6	A Oueſt.	2	Le vent Nort.	
	8	A Oueſt $\frac{1}{4}$ au Surroueſt.	$1\frac{1}{2}$	Le vêt Nort $\frac{1}{4}$ au Nordeſt.	
	10	A Oueſt $\frac{1}{4}$ au Surroueſt.	$1\frac{1}{4}$	Le vent Nornorroueſt.	
	12	Au Surroueſt $\frac{1}{4}$ à Oueſt.	2	Le vêt Norroueſt $\frac{1}{4}$ au Nort.	48.50. minutes.
	2	Au Surroueſt $\frac{1}{4}$ à Oueſt.	1	Au Norroueſt $\frac{1}{4}$ au Nort.	
	4	Au Surroueſt.	$\frac{3}{4}$	Le à Oueſt Norroueſt.	
	6	A Oueſt $\frac{1}{4}$ au Norroueſt.	$2\frac{1}{2}$	Le Nort.	
	8	A Oueſt.	$2\frac{1}{2}$	Le Nortnordeſt.	
	10	A Oueſt.	3	Le Nordeſt.	
	12	A Oueſt.	3	Le Eſt Nordeſt.	

Figure 14. Samuel de Champlain, *Traitté de La Marine* in: *Les Voyages de La nouvelle France…* (Paris: Louis Sevestre, 1632): 37. Compare with Figures 15 and 16.

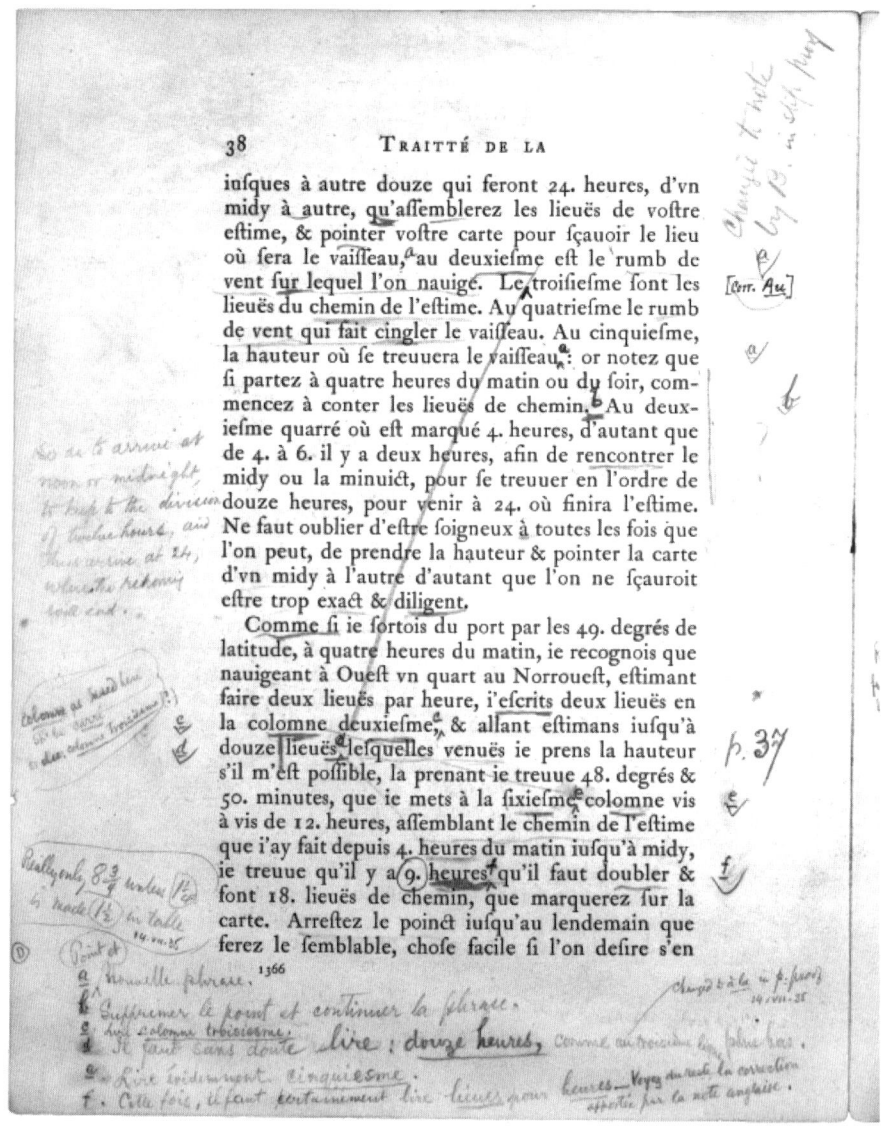

Figure 15. J. Home Cameron's editorial comments on the Laverdière collation of the *Traitté* page 38, covering approximately Champlain's original text given above as Figure 13.

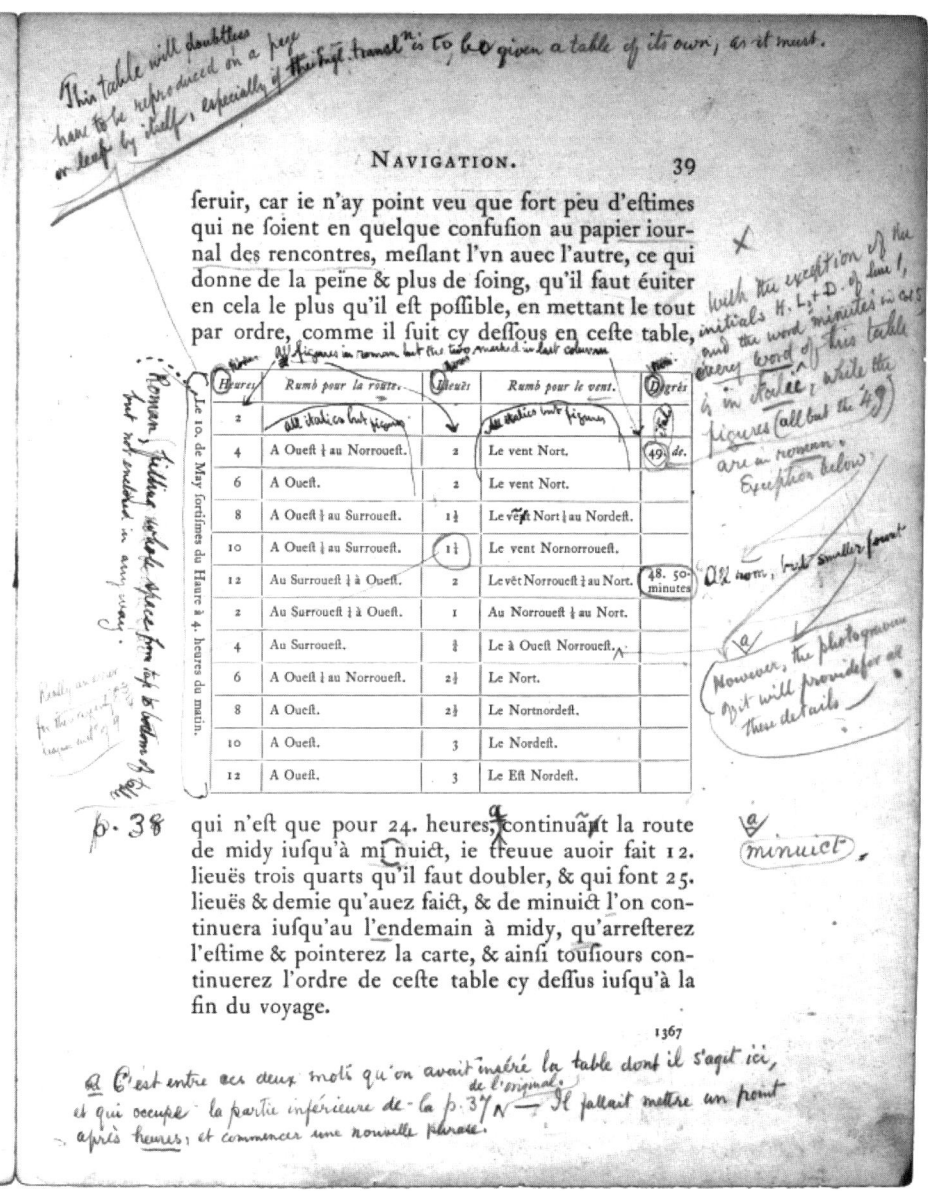

Figure 16. J. Home Cameron's editorial comments on the Laverdière edition of the *Traitté* page 39, covering approximately Champlain's original text given above as Figure 14.

Ganong, the cartographer of the editorial group, translated the tables for Champlain's maps of 1612, 1613 an 1632.[310]

Apart from a few Minutes of Council, the remaining correspondence regarding Volume VI is either missing or misfiled somewhere in the Champlain Society Papers. The volume was promised late of late in 1935 but did not appear until February 1936.[311] As late as November 1935, Cameron had found three Champlain letters he wanted to include; one to the King dated 1630 and two to Richelieu dated 1634 and 1635 (actually written in 1633).[312] These were forwarded to Biggar "for his final decision" and were included untranslated in the volume.[313] The only documents not included from the original text of *Les Voyages, 1632* were *Doctrine Chrestienne* by Father Jean de Brébeuf and *L'Oraison Dominicale* by Father Énemond Massé. The first of these is in Montagnais and French and the second in Montagnais only. Not having been written by Champlain, they were considered to be of marginal interest. They are however, of considerable interest to linguists and would only have added twenty pages to the volume.[314]

The cost of the last volume was as follows: Langton was paid $75 (26 March 1935) for translating the *Traitté*; Biggar was paid an instalment of $150 (12 September 1935), the remainder of his editorial fee of $215 (27 January 1936) and a bonus of $150 (29 February 1936); Cameron received $60; the Estate of LeSueur was sent $150 (17 August 1933); Julia Jarvis was paid $300 for the index (29 February 1936) and Spottiswoode $2462.92 for printing and shipping the books (10 November 1936) for a total cost of $3562.92.[315]

Winding up the Project

With volume VI safely in the hands of its members, The Champlain Society officially ended the project with a notice in their 1936 Annual Report:

> Since the last annual meeting of the Society, there has been issued to members the sixth and last volume of *Champlain's Works*. There has thus been brought to conclusion a project which was originally undertaken by the Society at the time of the Champlain tercentenary in Quebec in 1908, and which has been carried through under exceptional difficulties. It was not found possible to publish the first volume until 1922, fourteen years after the first plans were made; and another period of fourteen years has been found necessary to complete the whole work. For the supervision of the task, in which a number of scholars have collaborated, the thanks of the Society are owing especially to Dr. H. P. Biggar, the general editor. The Council of the

---

310 Champlain, *The Works*, ed. Biggar, Volume VI (1936), vii.
311 Ibid., item 67, Minute Books, 1926–1948. Minutes of 14 November 1934 and 28 May 1935.
312 Ibid., box 37, fol. 50, Cameron to Wallace 9 November 1935.
313 Ibid., item 67, Minutes of Council, 1926–1948, Minutes of 5 December 1935.
314 The Champlain Society did the same thing with Gabriel Sagard's *Grand Voyage* published in 1939, where they omitted the very important *Dictionaire de la Langve Hvronne*, the first detailed study of an Iroquoian language.
315 Ibid., item 15, General Ledger, 1906–1962.

Society could not have secured anyone better equipped than Dr. Biggar for the task of editing *Champlain*, and the wisdom of their choice is demonstrated in the volumes which are now in the hands of members.[316] Something should be said also about the contribution made to the volumes by Mr. H. H. Langton and Professor J. Home Cameron. Mr. Langton has done the greater part of the translation, and Professor Cameron has collated the French text. In doing this, Professor Cameron has examined and photographed various versions of Champlain's text found in libraries in both North America and Europe, and has spared no pains in order to establish as correct a text as possible. Mention should be made also of the very full index to the six volumes, which has been prepared by Miss Jarvis, the assistant secretary-treasurer of the Society.[317]

There was, however, the delicate and unsolved matter of the "Popular Edition," still promised on the reverse side of the title page of Volume VI. On January 17, 1928 Council had decided to buy the plates of *Champlain's Works* from Spottiswoode and ship them to Canada, so that the University of Toronto Press could publish the books at a later date. The Society, however, never followed through.[318] It will be recalled that besides the plates of the typeset texts, Spottiswoode Press had printed and stored on instruction from the Society an additional 600 copies of every illustration, map and photograph for every volume of *Champlain's Works* for a future popular edition. The subject came up again in 1938 when Langton wanted to discuss the popular edition but Council postponed the matter for a year.[319] The ledgers show that insurance was paid on the plates and illustrations for 1937 and 1938.[320] In return to queries from members, the popular edition kept on being promised, but often with qualifiers, such as:

> Council has not yet made any arrangements for the printing. For the sake of our subscribers, who have paid for the original volumes, we do not want to rush into print with a cheaper edition.[321]

The last time a popular edition was promised was on 11 August 1938, but "without the volume of plates and maps."[322] On 23 September 1938, Langton presented Council with an estimate from Spottiswoode of publication costs for printing 600 sets of six volumes each and the portfolio of maps:

---

316 This was the last mention of Henry Percival Biggar by The Champlain Society. He died on July 25, 1938, in Worplesdon, England. His death was not noted in the Minutes of the Society.
317 MS Coll. 50, item 67, Minute Books 1926–1948. *Report of the Annual Meeting of The Champlain Society*…(June 12, 1936): 3–4.
318 Ibid., Minutes of Council, 17 January 1928. The Champlain Society began publishing their regular series with the University of Toronto Press in 1931.
319 Ibid., Minutes of Council, 26 April 1938.
320 Ibid., item 14, Cash book (out-going) 1916–1962. Insurance for 1937, $8.53 and for 1938, $10.53.
321 Ibid., box 40, fol. 3, Jarvis to G. Stewart Cameron, 18 March 1937.
322 Ibid., fol. 5, Jarvis to Burbey, 11 August 1938.

> Printing and binding 200 sets (roughly) $6000; Printing 400 more sets (roughly) $665; Binding 400 more sets (roughly) $1600. Mr. Langton stated that the demand would in his opinion not justify the high cost of producing this new edition for sale to the public. He moved that the printer should be instructed to ship all moulds, plates etc. to this [Champlain Society, Toronto] office; and that no further action should be taken at present.[323]

Three days later Wallace wrote to Sir George Garneau[324] asking him if The Champlain Society was still obliged to publish the popular edition. The reply came almost immediately that there seemed to be no "...formal undertaking or conditions to this effect," and that he would "...advise his colleagues...to relieve your Society of any obligation in this respect."[325] (See Appendix VI). In December of the same year, Garneau's letter was read to Council with no further comments in the Minutes, it is probable however that Council members were asked to give the matter some serious thought.[326] They now had two pieces of information; first, the Battlefields Commission would not hold them to a "Popular Edition," and second, the cost of 600 sets would be about $8265, or $13.78 per set of six books ($2.30 per volume) including the portfolio of maps. By contrast, the average printing cost for 550 copies in the regular series from 1937 to 1948 was about $2,500 and if the Hudson's Bay Record Society volumes are included the cost was $2200 (see Tables 3 a, and 3 b), for an average printing cost of about $4.00 to $4.50 per volume. No basis was given for the opinion that there was little demand for the books, no effort was made to contact other presses to share publication costs against profits, no book companies were contacted that might take on the marketing of a popular edition and the Society had more than enough funds to publish the books on their own.[327] At the Council meeting on 27 September 1939:

> It was moved by Mr. Walker,[328] and seconded by Dr. Wrong and carried that in view of the fact that the Society has been released by the National Battlefields Commission from any obligation to bring out a popular edition of Champlain's Works, and in view of the high cost of freight at present, the Secretary be instructed to write to Spottiswoode, Ballantyne and

---

323 Ibid. item 67, Minutes of Council, 23 September 1938.
324 Sir George Garneau was Chairman of the National Battlefields Commission that had funded the Society for $5000 at the time of the Québec Tercentenary. He was a Vice President of The Champlain Society from 30 April 1921 until 10 May 1940.
325 Ibid. box 40, Fol. 17, Garneau to Wallace, 29 September 1938.
326 Ibid. item 67, Minutes of Council, 8 December 1938.
327 In October 1911, Langton had asked Burrows Bros. to undertake the sale of the popular edition. When they declined he contacted Arthur H. Clark Co. The reply from the latter company is not on record. Ibid. Box 48, fol. 17, Langton to Burrows Bros., 11 October 1911; fol. 18, Burrows Bros. to Langton, 6 November 1911, and Langton to Arthur H. Clark Co., 10 November 1911. Judging from Table 4, after 1932 the Society had the funds through their investments to easily cover the publication costs of a popular edition.
328 Harold C. Walker was Sir Edmund's youngest son. At the time of this meeting he was membership secretary.

Company asking the total cost of disposing of the plates, molds, etc. of the volumes, in such a way that they could not be made use of by anyone else.[329]

Appended to the Minutes is a letter by Lucien Pacaud, Secretary of the Battlefields Commission to Wallace stating formally that:

> I am pleased to inform you that the National Battlefields Commission, at its regular meeting held October 19 last, unanimously agreed to relieve the Champlain Society of any obligations to reprint a popular edition of the *Works of Samuel de Champlain*, as requested in your letter to Sir George Garneau of September 26 1938.

On 14 November, a payment of $71.80 was sent to Spottiswoode to dispose of the moulds and illustrations for the Champlain volumes,[330] and a few days later Wallace sent a letter of thanks to Pacaud thus ending the matter.[331]

What is one to conclude to this ending to The Champlain Society's only foray into a popular edition of its books? Sir Edmund Walker and others had hoped to create something lasting that the public could share after the Québec Tercentenary—a set of books that was fundamental to an understanding of Canada. What happened to Walker's lofty sentiments when the grant from the Battlefields Commission was announced?

> We ought to be conscious of the honour of being entrusted by the Government with the publication under our own imprint of the book that will remain for all time the memorial of the Tercentenary of the arrival of Champlain at Quebec.[332]

Of the 550 Champlain sets, usually 50 were set aside for gifts, review or editorial purposes, about 300 for individual members and 200 to libraries of which fewer than 100 were in Canada. In other words fewer than 100 sets were available to the Canadian public and even these were often in the rare book depositories of the libraries. Was the Society really trying to save money or was it a matter of trying to preserve "…a positive value in money in the future," for their books? Given the penchant of the Society at that time for a limited membership and restrictive reprint policies, one may be pardoned for thinking that the rare book collectors had taken over the Society and public education was no longer an important matter.

In his book *Lost Toronto*, the architectural historian William Dendy regretted the destruction of much of Toronto's architectural heritage, among it Sir Edmund Walker's

---

329 Ibid., item 67, Minutes of Council, 27 September 1939.
330 Ibid., item 14, Cash Book (out-going) 1916–1962. Another $15.11 was paid for insurance in 1939.
331 Ibid., box 40, fol. 17, Wallace to Pacaud, 27 November 1939.
332 Ibid., item 66, Minutes of Council, 6 April and Annual Meeting 5 May 1909.

house "Long Garth."[333] The year after Walker died, "Long Garth" was sold to Trinity College in the hope that the University of Toronto would preserve what was widely considered to be one of the finest examples of late Victorian architecture in the city. In 1969 the house was demolished to create a parking lot. In Dendy's words:

> This demolition—sponsored, as it was, by the university—was more than an act of vandalism. It must be considered a classic example of the philistinism that Walker had hoped to eradicate by supporting and encouraging that same university and its sister institutions.[334]

Much the same can be said of the destruction of the plates for *The Works of Samuel de Champlain* by the Society that Walker had created to bring these books before the general public.

---

333 William Dendy, *Lost Toronto* (Toronto: Oxford University Press, 1978), 167–71. "Long Garth" was at 99 St. George Street, on the east side of the street, between Bloor Street and Hoskin Avenue.
334 Ibid., p. 171.

CONCLUDING REMARKS

On the one hand, it is easy to criticize earlier editing procedures, or the lack of them, but even with the hindsight of a century, some astonishing errors and oversights were made that led to the delays and rancour that pervaded the Champlain project. On the other hand, the final product was a very significant contribution to scholarship that has stood the test of time remarkably well. The Champlain Society's *Works of Samuel de Champlain* is still the standard compilation and translation of the writings of the "Founder of New France."

Probably the single most important error made at the beginning of the project was not to undertake a feasibility study, including an examination of the variant Champlain texts and the adequacy of the Laverdière collation, followed by a realistic estimate of the time and funds necessary to carry the project to its completion. The Society went blindly into a complicated translating and publishing programme without establishing a common set of editorial principles until seven years into the project. Even after editorial procedures were developed they did not pertain to the French texts. These were left to the judgment of the general editor, Henry P. Biggar, who had significant differences with his translators on how to reproduce the original French texts and render them into English. Poor initial planning of course threw the entire time frame for the project into disarray, especially when it was discovered that the Laverdière collation was inadequate, and worse, when it took ten years to find a reliable scholar in J. Home Cameron who could do an expert job at collating the texts.

A second error made at the outset of the project was to assume that the translators could also act as content editors. Of the translator-editors, only William Ganong was competent to work as an editor on the area (Acadia) with which his texts dealt, and only he and Cameron felt that the original text should be reproduced as originally printed, "warts and all." John Squair was the only translator-editor willing to admit that he had no competence in the areas for which he was required to provide scholarly footnotes, except in matters pertaining to the French text. None but Ganong was competent to comment on Champlain's observations of the Native people he encountered, which in Ganong's case were the east coast Mi'kmaq. Champlain's writings on the culture of the Natives he contacted are at best indifferent, and say almost nothing about their non-material culture such as religion, political and social organization. In fact the editors were not even competent enough in these matters to note Champlain's deficiencies. Similar observations have been made about the ability of the editors to translate and edit "matters maritime" in Champlain's writings.[1]

Responsibility for the project rested with the executive and Council of the Society. Although these were competent administrators, business men and scholars, none at that time had much experience in collating, translating, editing and publishing original texts in any language other than English. Having committed themselves to two volumes per year, it is understandable that the Council and executive wanted to get the books into the hands of the members as quickly as possible, but in trying to do so, time demands were placed on the editorial staff that were often unrealistic in terms of the complicated material they were editing. This was especially so when increasingly the complex Champlain volumes had to fill publication gaps in the regular series, a rôle for which they were originally not intended. By placing time constraints on the editorial work to get the volumes published Biggar and the general editors of the Society were occasionally forced into having some texts typeset prematurely. This practice led to several sets of galleys, excessive corrections, increased trans-oceanic communication and eventually increased costs. Even as the project was nearing completion the Council and executive did not seem to understand the nature of the work that was involved; that the highest standards of collating, translating, editing and printing demand comprehensive planning, expertise, sufficient time and adequate amounts of money.

One can also understand, however, Council's insistence on tight budgeting, but when low financial resources became a recurring experience (see Table 4), thought should have been given much earlier than 1948 to raising the membership fees from $10 to $15. It was also unrealistic of the Society to persist so long in promising to deliver two volumes per year.[2] Except for the twelve years when the Hudson's Bay Company series was available, the Society never had the manuscripts or capacity to produce more than one volume per year (see Tables 2 a to 2 d). Spottiswoode, Ballantyne Press had suggested such structural changes during and after World War I, but the Council feared loss of members if they raised fees or cut the number of publications they promised to print. Another approach to increasing revenue might have been to expand the membership, but such a solution was unthinkable to those who regarded the Society as

---

1 Samuel Eliot Morison, *Samuel de Champlain, Father of New France* (Boston: Little, Brown and Company, 1972), 270.
2 Membership fees remained fixed at $10 from 1905 until they were raised to $15 in 1948. In 1952 the Society went officially to one volume per year.

a rare book club.³ Nothing illustrates the mindset that continued to promote a limited membership better than the cavalier attitude with which the popular edition of the Champlain project was terminated, through the deliberate destruction of the plates, illustrations and maps that had already been printed.

Finally, neither the executive nor the Council seemed to admit to themselves that those involved in the project had private and scholarly lives outside their obligations to The Champlain Society. To most of the editor-translators, the stipend they were being paid did not compensate them for the time, effort and irritation the project caused, and neither did the honour that was supposed to be attached to editing a book for the Society. Much of the irritation between the volume editors and the Council might have been avoided if direct links to the Council had existed.

The Champlain project was a success—not an unqualified success—but nevertheless a significant success. A few additions would have made it better. Cameron should have been permitted to write his essay on Champlain's use of French, on the location of the original texts and the problems of collating them. Biggar should have included a piece on the editorial procedures and someone, perhaps William Grant, on Champlain and his times. These topics (see Appendix III) had been raised as being important but interest slackened, time was no longer available and every additional page of text cost money. The project owed its success in large part to Cameron for collating the texts and checking the translations, Biggar for sticking with the project in spite of mounting criticism and increasingly poor health, and Langton for undertaking far more of the translation than anyone had originally planned.

Of these, J. Home Cameron was especially criticized throughout the project for almost single-handedly causing delays in producing the collated texts through his "obsession with accuracy that was pathological."⁴ There is little doubt that he could be an irritating person, especially for administrators, yet it was the collation of the French text that was probably the most significant achievement of the project. Cameron insisted on accuracy, which of course took time, and spent his own money to travel to Europe in order to search for variants in the texts. He also offered to use his stipend to pay for the delays he was causing and for a proper introduction to the texts, but the Society decided against this offer fearing further delays. For all his efforts in producing the six volumes, he was paid as much as Julia Jarvis was for compiling the index. He emerges in her reminiscences as almost a character out of a Gilbert and Sullivan operetta. In the annual reports and in various notations by Biggar in the *Works*, acknowledgement is made of Cameron's collation as a positive feature that gave the Champlain Society

---

3   Membership in the Society was eventually increased during the 1960s and opened completely to all applicants in the mid 1970s.
4   Julia Jarvis, "Speech, Part 2," p. 11.

edition stature, but of course no mention was made that he was successful in spite of the endless criticism by the executive and Council.

Henry P. Biggar's task was not an enviable one. His home, family and place of work were in England, as was the press with which the Society worked. He was rarely in Canada and therefore had to carry out all his editorial tasks by mail. It was inevitable that his location and that of the press would create delays in editing and in the publication schedule. Like all the translator-editors, his honorarium was inadequate for the extra work he put in such as the inclusion of newly discovered documents and extra translating. Worse, unlike some of the other translator-editors, he was not personally wealthy and as Chief Archivist for Canada in Europe held a poorly paid job. Corporate memories are often short as the executive and councillors change over time and misunderstandings become inevitable and difficult to reconcile by mail. Biggar had reservations about the project from the beginning, most of which were realized, but in spite of the temptation to quit when he felt he no longer had the confidence of the executive and Council, he had the strength of character to stay with the project to its end.

Hugh Langton was a competent translator and efficient administrator. His deep commitment to the Society that he had helped to found led him to take on any task that would further its objectives. In addition to translating about half the Champlain texts, including the very difficult *Traitté de la Marine*, he served as Treasurer of the Society from 1908–1912, 1923–34 and 1936–1947, and as president from 1934–1936.

A century has gone by since the Champlain project was conceived and set into motion. Over that time standards for editing historical texts have become more fully developed.[5] In view of the importance of generally accepted editing procedures, The Champlain Society now has a modern set of guidelines.[6] Over the years The Champlain Society edition of *The Works of Samuel de Champlain* has been regarded as the most authoritative text of Champlain's writings in both languages. In fact there has not been a new English scholarly edition and translation of his writings since the project ended in 1936. Nor is there a newly collated French text of all his writings edited to current scholarly standards. This is unfortunate because no edition of an historical text is ever definitive. Research on the early exploration, French settlement and Native people of Canada has made enormous advances since the Champlain project ended.

When The Champlain Society was founded, it was hoped that the books of the Society would have "a positive value in the future." Occasionally one of the 550 sets of

---

5   Jennifer S.H. Brown, "Documentary Editing: Whose Voices?" and Laura Millar Coles, "Looking Backward; Reaching Forward: The Champlain Society and Documentary Publishing." *Occasional Papers of The Champlain Society*, no. 1 (Toronto: The Champlain Society, 1992): 1–14, 15–35.
6   Germaine Warkentin, "The Champlain Society Guidelines for Editing Canadian Historical Texts." http://www.champlainsociety.ca/cs_publications-advice.htm.

The Works of Samuel de Champlain comes up for sale. In December 2005, antiquarian book dealers listed two sets at $1,700 and $2000 US. The 1971-limited edition reprint by the University of Toronto Press generally fetches $450 to $550 US. These prices reflect not only a scarce commodity but also a compelling story by a great man who laid the foundations of Canada.

The Champlain project encapsulates the history of the Society in many respects: the preparation and production of a limited edition of beautifully printed volumes consisting of well-edited texts with a pertinent introduction, of important books and documents relating to Canada's history. Some of the difficulties encountered in the Champlain project are still common today, such as unexpected delays in volume editing and battles over cost to produce high quality publications without exceeding the financial capabilities of the Society. Other difficulties have been overcome through more clearly defined editing procedures, production facilities that are now in Canada and much better communications between the Society and its editors. The limited membership that was once a problem for the Society now no longer exists. Instead, the principal challenge for the Society has become the expansion of its membership in a world of changing mass communications.

Is there still a rôle for beautifully produced historical texts such as Champlain's *Works*, in an age where a simple Internet connection can bring the originals to a computer screen? We are certain that Sir Edmund Walker would have answered in the affirmative and that he would have been pleased to hear that the Society has embarked on a new edition of Champlain's *Works*, one that will definitely be sold to the public.

APPENDICES

Appendix I

ADDRESS BY B. E. WALKER, ESQ., TO *THE CANADIAN CLUB, OTTAWA*, FEBRUARY 4TH, 1904

In the last ten or fifteen years there has been a great growth in our confidence as to the solidarity of the scattered provinces and territories now comprised in Canada. We have at last come to believe that we are to be a nation. I am aware that there are those who will deny the propriety of using such a word to describe our political condition. But the Scotch are a nation, the Irish are a nation, and I shall speak of Canada as a nation. We are rapidly developing a great confidence in our future, and great confidence in the future of a young country is apt to take the form of boasting about it. We talk constantly about the size of Canada, its vast natural resources, its immense potency in producing natural wealth, and we take credit for all this just as if we Canadians had created Canada. Instead of this we should remember every day of our lives, with bowed heads, that Canada was made for us and for our heirs, and that we are merely stewards for posterity, answerable as we do well or ill by Canada. This confidence, however, as to what Canada will do *for us* is an agreeable change from the fears expressed by the doubting Thomases of the past, but it should always be accompanied by a grave and reverent sense of what we should do for Canada—a very different sort of problem from what Canada should do for us.

Before we approach in detail the duty of Canadians to Canada, let us set forth what will constitute success in the development of Canada; what will be a satisfactory fulfilment of our duty to Canada. An answer in a broad sense is not difficult. To produce that condition of national life which will support many, but not too many, millions in comfortable but not too affluent circumstances; a civilization which gives as much liberty as is good for us; a satisfactory division among the various classes of men and women of the labour to be performed and of the rewards to flow there from; and a full recognition of the arts, and of learning in its highest forms and for its own sake.

Many other qualities may be added. I have purposely avoided reference to national morals and politics because in such a Utopia as I have sketched the moral conditions would certainly be satisfactory. We shall not arrive at such a Utopia, but surely it is something like what we should aim at, and "a man's reach should exceed his grasp, or what's a heaven for?"

Our honoured statistician, Mr. Johnson, tells us that Canada is about 3,500 miles in extent from east to west, and about 1,400 miles from north to south; that its southern boundary of about 3,000 miles is about 1,400 miles of water and 1,600 miles of land; and that its entire content is 3,750,000 square miles. He divides the southern part geographically into an eastern area of woodlands, a middle area of prairies, and a western area of mountains. The sea coast on the Atlantic, the Arctic, Hudson Bay, and the Pacific is greater than that of any other nation. Its inland lakes and rivers are the wonder of the world. Its forests, covering the whole of the Atlantic and Pacific areas, and stretching between these areas through the northern parts of Quebec, Ontario, Manitoba, and Saskatchewan, and northward to the limit of vegetation, make a draft upon the imagination to which few of us can respond. I do not, however, intend to describe Canada. I only wish to startle your imagination as to what it means to be a Canadian, and to have come into possession of a life interest in such a domain.

All along our history there have been men who believed intensely in the future of the part of Canada which they called home, and some of them have dreamed of a larger Canada; but few have dared to think of her as a nation destined some day to wield great influence as part of the governing power of the British Empire, or as an independent power, which latter God forbid. The love of Papineau and Lafontaine for Quebec; of William Lyon Mackenzie and Robert Baldwin for Upper Canada; of Joseph Howe for Nova Scotia, is enough, whether we regard as well or ill their struggles with the bureaucrats of Quebec, or with the family compacts of Upper Canada and Nova Scotia. The wider view of the Fathers of Confederation was, after all, made possible only by the struggles of these earlier heroes for representative government and home rule.

It would take too much time to trace the steps of our intensely interesting history from the first landings at Cape Breton, Sable Island, Annapolis, and in the St. Lawrence, through that romantic time of geographical discovery, missionary zeal, and fur-trading, ending not in the abandonment of what so often seemed a hopeless struggle, but in the turning over of the problem by the militant and religious enthusiasts of France to the domestic and colonizing Briton; to tell of the struggles for parliamentary government, and then for representative government; of the hopes and fears leading to the great plunge, confederation—that effort to link together provinces on both oceans, with hardly an interest in common and with gigantic natural obstacles between; of the building of our first great transcontinental railway and of our fears that it would not pay operating expenses; of our dreadful nights of despairing anxiety lest frost should prove that our prairies were practically worthless; of our mistaken feeling of dependence upon the United States as the only market for many of our products.

But when, since confederation, things were at their darkest, many of us repeated over and over again that old English proverb—"It's dogged as does it." We did not falter, and we talked as big as we knew how.

And when the railway began to pay dividends, and the farm boys who had left Ontario for Manitoba began to come back for a holiday every winter in their coon skins, when we began to see that the unfriendliness of the United States had been a blessing in disguise, then began to throb through the brain of one Canadian after another the conviction that as *one* nation, with possibilities beyond calculation, we had won.

Now that it can be done so readily, every Canadian should read the history of his country, both the period of romance and that of political and industrial development. Without doing so he can never understand how precious is the trust which has come down to him. Let him also study the maps and survey reports, the blue-books—indeed anything that will cause him to understand Canada as a physical problem.

In discussing the possibilities of the development of Canada and our duty towards it, we must first consider it industrially, not only because that is the aspect which inevitably comes first, but because it is right that it should be so. Man's first right is to live. In the older world, society does not expect those members of the community who are literally seeking bread to be influenced by high considerations in their struggle for life, and we cannot remember too often that the men who settled this country and the men who are settling the western part of it now, came in almost every case seeking bread—bread for themselves and their children. Perhaps no one who has not seen a first effort in the bush where the settler is engaged in his furious onslaught on nature in order to clear the land wherefrom he expects to support his family, can fully understand why a young country in its early efforts at civilization is so intensely materialistic and so profligate in destroying natural resources merely for gain. We are old enough to have made excellent game laws, but none of us expect a settler who in Muskoka needs meat, or on a salmon river needs fish, to respect these laws. We must not fail to recognize that no destruction of what nature has provided is profligate if it is necessary to sustain life. But when men have attained comfort and go on destroying merely for gain what nature has provided, new considerations arise, and we have the right to ask whether such destruction is hurtful or not to the future of the nation; whether, indeed, we have the right to accumulate unnecessary wealth now by the destruction of what may be necessary for the mere bread of generations to come.

The natural resources to come under consideration may be roughly divided into three groups:

1st. Where we reap but do not sow, and, having once reaped, cannot replace. Our coal and other mines are examples.

2nd. Where we reap as we sow. In older countries this would be true of wheat and other cereals. But in Canada this is not quite be true even of wheat. From virgin soils we may reap twenty-five or thirty bushels of wheat to the acre, which in a few years may fall on the same lands to fifteen or twenty bushels. Here to the extent of the surplus we have reaped without sowing.

3rd. Where we may reap for a time without sowing, but only at the expense of posterity. Our forests and fisheries are examples.

In the treatment of our wheat fields in the North-West, our forests and fisheries everywhere, we are little better than barbarians, and I ask—How is enlightened sentiment as to our duty to be created? How can we make every Canadian understand that our precious position as the grower of the best wheat in North America can only be maintained by our putting back into the earth the constituents which have been used in growing our crops? How can we make every Canadian understand that except where the land under the trees is worth more as a farm than as a forest, we should replace every full-grown tree we cut down by what will eventually produce another? And how can we make every Canadian sufficiently realize the enormous value we have in our fisheries to make him press for such an enlightened policy on the part of our government as will ensure these food supplies for ever? How, indeed, can we make him understand that if we take what it is possible and wise for us to replace and do not replace it, we are committing a crime against our own children?

We are doubtless destined to remain a democracy, and however little or much we may admire it, we may as well make up our minds to shape our future with reference to the fact that we shall continue to be governed by a democracy. One of the inherent defects of democracy seems to be that our rulers and our newspapers only represent the average of the intelligence and the morality of our people. In the service of the government and on the judicial bench men are needed with unusual ability and with unselfish devotion, and no services in society should so readily claim both qualities; but democracy will not pay for expert ability and does not expect unusual devotion to duty. We must, I fear, admit that we are rarely proud of our political conditions, of our civil service system, or of our press. We are only proud of the individuals in politics, civil service, or the press, who are strong enough to rise above the level made by the average. But if present tendencies are not checked what must be the outcome? No sincere, sober, thoughtful citizen of the United States is really satisfied with what democracy has done for his country. Have we not, indeed, terrible evidence in the United States as to the lack of any peculiar virtue in democracy, *per se,* as a form of government? What, then, are we to do to avert the same result? Is it not clear that we must vigilantly guard against the inherent weakness of democracy by steadily lifting up the average of our own intelligence and morals? We must set before the young other ideals than gross materialism—mere money-making. We must save and increase such good qualities as tend to differentiate us from the United States. If we act as if the almighty dollar is the end, it will be the end, and this country will become a huge oligarchy dominated by selfish industrial interests, which will easily, by machine politics, register from time to time a vote supposed to express the wishes of the people, but really recording the determinations of the oligarchy. Whatever we may do we may be sure that in respect to virtue our government will fairly reflect the average virtue of the people.

When we turn to our newspapers we at once realize their tremendous influence. I have so many good friends among the newspaper men of Canada that I do not wish to be misunderstood, and I know that I am about to enter on dangerous ground. I suppose it is because of the violent manner in which politicians abuse each other in Parliament that newspapers abuse all politicians not of the party for which they stand, and misrepresent, more or less, all that these politicians say or do. The effect of this attempt to eliminate from an opponent all that is good, and to exaggerate all that is bad, is not so much to deceive the people as to leave them uncertain as to what to believe. Perhaps this is one of the main reasons for the cynicism regarding public and private virtue which is common to almost the entire press, and is much too frequently met with in our young people. And certainly this tendency to exaggerate all statements of fact must have a most unfortunate result on the veracity of people generally. How can the public as a whole have much regard for the truth when they realize that newspapers in making a case for their party do not hesitate to colour the truth just as it suits their argument? I wonder if I dare say anything about the personal and the social column? I have not hesitated to do so elsewhere in the presence of reporters and they have applauded what I said. Indeed, they must have their own opinion of the class of people who use these columns in order to exploit themselves, the men politically and the women socially. Surely nothing could be more shocking, more horrid than this vulgar desire for notoriety. But, unfortunately, all these objectionable features exist because the people who read the newspapers desire to find them there. My purpose to-day is not to blame the newspapers for giving the people what they want. It is to blame the people for not wanting better newspapers.

Nothing can, of course, be more important in the upbuilding of our intellectual and moral conditions than our educational system, but here, too, the inherent defects of democracy are most noticeable. That in a new country we should have badly-equipped and badly-paid teachers is perhaps inevitable, and time will surely cure these evils. As long as there is rapid development in new parts of Canada and continued expansion in many old parts, professional men of all kinds, and especially school teachers, will be demanded in too great numbers to make it possible to be very particular as to the qualifications of many of them. I do not, however, wish to discuss our educational system, but certain effects upon it of democracy. Unfortunately, in a democracy the idea of the average man seems to be to get as much as possible from the state without paying for it, and this is particularly noticeable in our educational system. As a natural result of this the politicians are willing to keep on enlarging the scope of national education, until it is hard to guess what our system will lead to. Doubtless, we shall eventually, at the, expense of the state, examine the eyes and teeth of the children, and do many more things of a similar nature. One of the worst features, however, is the prevalent idea that the purpose of education is merely to fit the pupil to earn his living. I must not be understood as objecting to technical schools. Night schools of all kinds for those who cannot take a regular school course are to the last degree admirable, and technical schools as a superstructure to ordinary schools are much needed; but I do not believe in any system of education which does not make men think and which does not create a love of learning for its own sake. To spell, to write, to cipher, to think intelligently, to be able to hear evidence with an open mind, to speak and act like a gentleman—these are by far the most important elementary qualities in a system of education. Indeed, character and the power to think are the great end, and not the making of plumbers or of carpenters. We cannot make men fit to govern a nation, we cannot make patriotic thoughtful citizens, simply by technical education.

What I have said has been mainly suggestive. The theme is too great for a single address, and I have already spoken too long. I have asked many questions as to our future. Allow me to restate some of them.

We shall undoubtedly succeed industrially; but are we to be a cultured people? We are to be rich—are we to be wise?

Possibly in a generation or two, when the United States shall have reached her limit of productiveness of food for export, and we shall largely have taken her place, we shall be among the first in commerce. Shall we also be among the first in arts and letters? And unless we attain this distinction, shall we have succeeded as a nation?

Before the end of the present century we shall probably be one of the most powerful nations, or one of the most powerful parts of the British Empire. Shall we also be a just nation? Are we to develop so as to be what Great Britain alone now is—a nation that can be trusted to govern subject peoples justly?

We are to be a democracy; but will that be a guarantee of freedom or merely government by an oligarchy?

Perhaps much that I have said may cause you to imagine that I am by nature a pessimist. Far from it; indeed, regarding Canada there can be few who are greater optimists. But optimism must be ballasted with common sense. The wise optimist expects trouble, but looks upon all trouble as mere detail, and plans in advance to meet it. I am so proud of my country and so confident of my countrymen that I look for the best results; but my ideal of what we should eventually become is so high that all conditions which deter instead of aiding our progress are irritating.

We are just beginning to be on trial before the other nations of the world. Surely boastfulness is not the character to show them, but humbleness and earnestness. Still, we who have sprung from the best nations, with the highest ideals and noblest traditions, who live in a country that breeds hardy men—we who have held this great out-post for the British Empire—should not be satisfied with half-greatness, but should aim to be greatest among the great. And we cannot become a great nation without developing national character with decided moral greatness. We have not developed great moral qualities as yet, and there is enough wrong in our country already to make us anything but vain of our stewardship thus far.

We can never hope to achieve real national success unless we aspire beyond material interests to those higher elements of civilization which alone can make a nation great.

Appendix II

PATRIOTISM AND HISTORY BY PROF. CHAS W. COLBY
[*PROCEEDINGS OF THE CANADIAN CLUB*, TORONTO, MARCH 6, 1905, PP. 107–116]

The subject upon which I wish to address you is suggested partly by the aims of your club and partly by the nature of my own profession. It is well known all over Canada that in this place you not only eat excellent lunches, but discuss with serious intent matters which are of consequence to the whole Dominion. Patriotism is, indeed, the very cornerstone of your institution, the motive force of your society, the firm bond which holds you together. Nor, on the other hand, can the student of history neglect patriotism, which has so long been one of the most potent factors in the life of mankind. It must be confessed that at times both patriotism and history have been made a target for innuendo. In the eighteenth century, for example, Walpole uttered his famous sarcasm, "Read me anything but history, for history must be false," and Walpole's contemporary, Dr. Johnson, was equally severe on patriots when he declared that patriotism was the last refuge of a scoundrel. Doubtless there have been in the past many slipshod and lying historians, many selfish and insincere patriots; but for the present we may pass these by as I wish to deal only with sound history and genuine patriotism.

I have heard it urged more than once that the rank and file of Canadians would be more loyal citizens if patriotism were more carefully taught as a lesson in the days of boyhood. We are not infrequently reminded of the efforts which are made throughout the United States to instil love of country at the same moment with the elements of spelling. The flag waving over the schoolhouse, the exercises in elocution which revive the perorations of Patrick Henry, of Webster and of Lincoln, the services on Decoration Day and the transformation of the old New England Fast Day into Patriot's Day are among the things which must certainly tend to strike the youthful imagination. Outside Japan there is probably no part of the globe where national pride and enthusiasm are stronger than in the United States. Those in Canada who have observed this phenomenon and who hold it up for our emulation often speak of the part that it played in the creation of loyalists by the elementary text book of history. The whole argument resolves itself to this: Firstly, that a somewhat militant spirit of patriotism is desirable; and, secondly, that the historical manual should be used as a means of setting forth in picturesque and convincing fashion the facts which help to glorify the national past or the arguments which go to defend the national cause. Those who repeat with unction the sentiment, "our country, right or wrong," would doubtless be content to have a colored, one-sided version of the national annals presented to children in public schools through the medium of the elementary manual.

Now what is the attitude of the professional historian toward this state of mind, towards this form of patriotism? I need hardly say that during the past two generations an attempt has been made by leading students of the past to render the investigation and the writing of history impartial, colorless and scientific. The ideal is that the historian should have, so far as is humanly possible, the disinterestedness of the dead; that he should not set forth the results of his researches with a view to justifying any special cause, or even to vindicate the record of his own ancestors. The spirit of exact science has so far impressed itself upon historians as to make them shun exaggeration, keep themselves in the background and let the facts, after they have been rigidly determined, speak for themselves. Truth is the ideal—not patriotism, nor even religion.

One, of course, is familiar with many lapses from this high standard on the part of famous historians in recent times. Mommsen, when exalting the character of Julius Caesar; Droysen, when defending the memory of Frederick the Great; Von Sybel, when describing the establishment of the German Empire; and Treitschke, when reviling England, illustrate the pressure of human infirmity even among the Germans, who are the reputed authors of historical science. Yet the ideal, though difficult of realization, remains, and with the most reputable historians it has become a point of self-respect to guard against the expression of one's own personal feeling. I can illustrate what I mean by reference to the letters of Bishop Stubbs which have just been published. In his familiar correspondence, Stubbs was by no means reticent in expressing his views on historical subjects. Naturally, his mind had a strong bias; or perhaps one ought rather to say he entered the world with the convictions of a High Churchman and a Tory. In one of his letters to Freeman he states that it is quite impossible for a Dissenter to write a good history of England. In politics, academic and national, his views were expressed frequently in verses and epigrams. During the war of Italian independence, he was strongly opposed to the cause of United Italy, and says whatever he [can] on behalf of the Austrians. Yet, when it came to writing his Constitutional History of England, Stubbs, without obliterating his own personality, masked his prepossessions completely. There is no one now living who is more familiar with that great book than Prof. F. W. Maitland, and, in his admirable article on Stubbs in the English Historical Review, Maitland states that he could not have formed any opinion from a most careful reading of the three volumes as to how Stubbs would have voted. "If I had hazarded a guess," he concludes, "it would have been the wrong-one."

Under modern conditions, then, it would be difficult to find a decent historian who would undertake to write a school manual with the fixed intent of justifying- the national cause, - that is to say, of presenting part of the truth as though it were the whole truth, against which nothing could be urged. I have referred already to the patriotism of people in the United States. There is still current the belief that this feeling is stimulated by the version given in school histories of the Revolutionary War and the war of 1812. But, so far as I can make out, after some investigation of the subject, there is good ground to suppose that in the Eastern States and throughout the Middle West the standard text books are not seriously warped by patriotic prejudice. I looked into this matter at the time of the Venezuela incident with a view to preparing an article on the subject, but found that there would be little ground for stricture. And, when I wrote to Mr. W. P. Garrison, the editor of the *Nation*, asking that he would collect for me ten or fifteen of the manuals on English and American History which were then most in vogue, he replied that he would do so gladly if I wished, but expressed his own surprise on finding how fair in tone the average manual of American History now was in dealing with these subjects. In going outside the field of manuals, it is really States which is somewhat hostile to Great Britain. But whether or not amusing to see how American writers like the late Moses Coit Tyler and Prof. Hart and Mr. Henry Adams write on the events of 1775 from what seems like the English standpoint; whereas Sir George Trevelyan and Mr. Justin McCarthy approach the same subject in mood of sympathy with the revolted Colonies.

The Middle West is frequently regarded as a part of the United [States] this be the fact, I am quite convinced that the historians are not responsible for keeping alive the memory of ancient grudges. For example, in a recent book on modern history, Prof. W. M. West, of the University of Minnesota, takes for the motto of his chapter on the British Empire this saying of Admiral Dewey: "After many years of wandering I have come to the conclusion that the mightiest factor in the civilization of the world is the imperial policy of England." Here, certainly, there is no note of hostility, nor has historical criticism won any more signal triumph during the past twenty-five years than is represented by the increased candor of the school histories now used throughout the civilized world.

We all recognize, I imagine, the existence of patriotism under two forms: Under the lower form of beating the big drum or waving the bloody flag; and under the higher form of doing something for one's country. The Countess von Arnim, with delicious satire, touches off this quality in the average Prussian of to-day. Elizabeth in Rugen alludes to some Prussian victory of which her maid, Gertrude, is profoundly ignorant, but the latter rises to the occasion and on this reference to a Prussian victory looks as one " who inwardly swells." Of course we are all subject to the same sort of feeling more or less, but if, in Canada, we had less to say about our illimitable resources and worked with steadfast purpose to have the most irreproachable politics in the world, our patriotism would not be slumbering the while. Nor is the connection of history with the higher patriotism, less close than it is with the screaming of the eagle or the roaring of the lion.

There is no country of the world where, so far as my own knowledge goes, a sounder type of patriotism is to be met with than exists in Switzerland. The connection between the Alps and the spirit of freedom is very old, but the modern Swiss do not live upon the reputation of Morgaten, Naefels and Sempach. It would be a breach of truth to say that Swiss history is without its grave blemishes. The willingness with which, for example, the peasants of the forest cantons sold their swords for centuries to the highest bidders justified the old proverb, *Pas d'argent, pas de Suisses;* while the government of subject lands like the Argan, Ticino and Vand by the confederates was nothing short of tyrannical. But the Switzerland of to-day, stimulated by its noble traditions and profiting by its experience of past errors, is really an object lesson to the world. It has twice been my privilege to attend the Swiss *Lands gemeinde,* that ancient assembly still existing in seven cantons, which represents the ancient German freedom in its purest form. Freeman begins his "Growth of the English Constitution" with a fervid description of the gathering in which the men of Uri, year by year, from the first Sunday in May, make their own laws and choose their own magistrates. The picture as he draws it is by no means over colored so far as the dignity of the occasion and the emotions of the spectator are concerned. It is indeed a solemn moment when one stands "face to face for the first time with freedom in its purest and most ancient form." Obviously, this kind of gathering does not suffice for the needs of a large democratic community and in the more populous cantons it has been given up, but apparently the public spirit of Berne and Zurich is not less than that of Uri and Glarns. Switzerland is a land of peace and yet a country which probably possesses the best militia force of its size anywhere. Swiss neutrality has been guaranteed by every one of the great powers, but the republic, with France and Germany for neighbours, does not place too much reliance in promises. At the *Landsgemeinde* of Uri each citizen appears with his sword at his side—the sword which the law compels him to wear and forbids him to draw. This, however, is a mere survival. Of more practical moment is the regulation which requires every citizen to have a rifle and 40 rounds of ammunition constantly in his house. The Swiss militia is the male part of the nation and can be mobilized for the defense of the frontier at a moment's notice. Nowhere is target practice a more popular sport. Whether he goes to the rifle range or to the polling booth on Sunday afternoon, the Swiss citizen feels that he is performing his civic duties and these are, for the most part, discharged in a spirit worthy of the day.

I refer to Switzerland merely for the sake of illustration and because it is a land where people, without being aggressive, know how to protect themselves, as in civic life they know how to govern themselves without recourse to wholesale bribery and corruption. Such public spirit as is displayed in this small and vigorous land, which was the first part of Europe outside isolated towns, to escape from feudalism, must be encouragement to those who believe that the noise of patriotism is often in inverse ratio to the emotion.

There is a phrase which Mr. Morley may have used when addressing you last fall, as it is one he is rather fond of. He says that he is often accused of being the friend of every country but his own. The historian, likewise, in trying to place things in proper perspective, must guard himself against this same charge. So far as Canada is concerned, history ought to have a large part in the national life—indeed, a much larger part than it has at present. Perhaps I can express what I mean best under the form of a slight anecdote. A classmate of my own has since become an eminent mining engineer, whose duties take him to many parts of the world. For six years he lived continuously in an important quarter of the British Empire, which I shall not name, because the allusion to it may seem rather disparaging. On being asked for a general criticism of the colony in question, as compared with Canada, he replied at once, "The trouble with that country is that it has no history," and he proceeded to show how in his opinion the absence of standards and traditions affected the life of the colony to its detriment. The speaker had no interest in history whatever—or at least only the interest which all educated men have in the subject—but his diagnosis of fundamental shortcomings took this form. In Canada we certainly have a history which is worth honoring, and the great pity is that so far we have done so little to exploit it. Instead of talking grandiloquently about our past, the truer patriotism would seem to point toward a closer investigation of it.

Let me try to express what I mean a little more fully. A few years ago, the late H. D. Traill edited a "Social History of England," and more recently M. Ernest Lavisse of the French Academy has edited a co-operative history of France. The same sort of thing has been done for America by Justin Winsor in his "Narrative and Critical History," while much of Winsor's work is being done over at the present moment by a group of scholars in the United States under the direction of Prof. Hart. But, speaking frankly, in the case of Canada the materials on which a good co-operative history can alone be founded do not exist. I feel pretty sure that neither Mr. Bain nor Prof. Wrong nor Mr. Langton will gainsay me at this point. A few weeks ago, I had .a conversation with Dr. Doughty, the Dominion archivist, regarding a project for a co-operative history of Canada, to be brought out in connection with the Champlain celebration at Quebec in 1908. Whether such a work will be attempted is a separate question, but I think most experts will agree with Dr. Doughty in thinking that anything at present attempted on these lines would be of a purely provisional character. In a broad sense all historical writing is provisional, since each age refuses to be content with the historiography left it by its predecessors. In the case of Canada, however, any co-operative history undertaken at the present time would be of the most tentative character, and for this reason, - the monograph stage has not, with us, as yet been passed through.

One need not attempt to define at any great length the relations which should exist between the monograph—or special study dealing with a particular incident—and the national history. It is obvious that the latter must cover an immensely larger area and draw its materials from the data accumulated by many individuals through a long process of intensive research. Historians are sometimes inclined to ask whether it is possible any longer to do the work of co-ordination at all. Personally, I believe that every generation needs histories written for itself, however surely they may be doomed to eventual oblivion. Still, the national historian can achieve nothing which is at all satisfactory until a host of subjects have been investigated with minute and scrupulous care by patient delvers. President Woodrow Wilson, of Princeton, has recently urged the historical specialist to work in the spirit of the artist, turning out cameos which will be as much prized as large canvases. It would be ridiculous to deny that the literature of Canadian history is wholly lacking in good monographs. Books like Rochemonteix's "Jesuits," Lorin's "Frontenac," Doughty's "Siege of Quebec," and Biggar's "Early Trading Companies," speak eloquently to the contrary.

Still, an enormous amount of pioneer work must be done before a bibliography of Canadian history can show any such results as are represented by a little book like Channing and Hart's "Guide to American History."

This statement brings me to a topic of practical interest—the topic which, indeed, of all others, should receive most attention from such patriots as desire to do something for the cause of Canadian History. We need to have at Ottawa a well-endowed and creditable Archives Department. I do not breathe a word against the late archivist, Mr. Brymner, nor the present archivist, Dr. Doughty. No one in this Dominion has a more sincere or disinterested zeal for the expansion and improvement of the archives than Dr. Doughty. No one is prepared to strive more unflaggingly than he to gather, arrange and edit our national records. The situation is an extremely simple one. In the past we have neglected an important duty by treating the Archives in a purely incidental fashion. For many years past the main affiliation of this department has been agricultural. The time has come to render it *cultural* in a broad and national sense.

Were it necessary to make a formal plea, the nexus of argument would run thus: Theoretically, at least, we all desire that there should be sound and learned histories of Canada. These cannot be prepared until a large number of special topics have been investigated with minute care. Owing to the present limitation of the national archives, the work of preparing good monographs is extremely difficult and costly. Therefore, one must conclude that the only sound policy is to collect and arrange these original materials without recourse to which the historian will be making a large waste of his time in writing on Canadian subjects at all. I do not pretend that the Government should be asked to collect everything. If it made this attempt it might have the same experience which the Patent Office of the United States had in the matter of models. The original design of Congress was to preserve a model of each patented machine or appliance, but about twenty years ago a crisis was reached. It then became clear that if this rule were adhered to it would be necessary to roof over the whole district of Columbia, and no one recommended that course. So, in the case of our own archives. Not every kind of record can be preserved by the Dominion Government at Ottawa, but certain great categories of documents ought to be brought together and made thoroughly accessible.

Our backwardness in comparison with other civilized countries might be brought out by some extremely graphic statistics. For example, the annual appropriation made for the Archives Department has not until now exceeded $12,000. For next year I understand that the grant is likely to be $20,000. But the single state of Wisconsin spends $45,000 a year on its Historical Society—a sum which at the next session of the Legislature will probably be raised to $55,000. Now the population of Wisconsin is about one-third the population of Canada, and such history as it has to spend its money on is largely an overflow from Canadian history. That State is represented in the statuary hall of the capitol at Washington by a figure of Pere Marquette, and those whom they delight to honour in orations are the *coureurs de bois,* or explorers like La Salle, Du Luth and Hennepin. If Wisconsin can afford to lay out $45,000 per annum on history, we surely, with thrice the population and a far richer history can afford to spend whatever is necessary in collecting and arranging the chief materials required for original research. As a matter of fact, not more than $45,000 a year would be needed, unless the publication of documents were attempted.

I have taken Wisconsin as a shining example of the liberality which is shown by the Western States in fostering historical studies, and I may supplement the statistics already given by saying that in the whole area covered by the United States between 400 and 500 historical societies exist. Most of these are active organizations and many of them, besides owning much valuable property, issue a series of publications.

Europe, however, furnishes us with even more valuable precedents than are to be drawn from the United States. Take Great Britain alone. I say nothing of the work done by a multitude of learned societies—the Selden Society, the Surtees Society, the Camden Society, the Hakluyt Society, the Spottiswoode Society, the Maitland Club, the Pipe Roll Society, and a whole host of similar organizations supported by private effort. But what should we do at this time of day without those publications, the expense of which has been borne by Government? I refer to the Rolls Series for mediaeval history, the Calendars of State Papers for the Tudor and Stuart periods, the reports of the Historical MSS. Commission for private archives. France, in certain respects, has been even more lavish, for ever since 1839 it has supported at public expense the Ecole des Chartes, an institution wherein many of the best mediaevalists now living have been trained. Within a few months Mr. C. H. Firth, the new professor of history at Oxford, has been pleading in his inaugural lecture that Oxford should begin to train men for historical work as they have long been trained in France at this state supported Ecole des Chartes. Equally decisive examples are afforded by the action of other continental states—not only by the first-class powers like Germany, Austria, and Italy, but [also] by Switzerland, Holland, Belgium and the Scandinavian lands. Even Spain has a fine new archives building at Madrid, though the most precious documents which the Spaniards possess are lodged in a desolate and almost deserted castle at Simancas, where a group of functionaries spend the winter months, huddled around a red hot stove, smoking cigarettes in a building that is far from being fire proof.

To take the case of Canada alone. In this country we spend nothing on national education, and, even if we had more money and a better disposition to spend, grave difficulties would confront us when we came to the details of the expenditure. We spend nothing on literature—apart from the up-keep of the Parliamentary Library. We cut down the grant to the Geological Survey, until in the opinion of many it is quite inadequate. As for the archives, the prospect is better now than it has been for some time past. The appropriation is going up from $12,000 to $20,000, and a new building is being provided. But the whole subject must be approached in a broad-minded spirit by legislators and the public if we are not to fall behind many smaller and less wealthy communities. Speaking quite candidly, we are pretty far behind already, and the question hinges less upon the task of holding our own than on the more difficult one of making up lost time.

I do not wish to be regarded as taking the tone of a pessimist or as disparaging, the best contributions which have already been made to Canadian history. A fourth form boy with a taste for etymology was once asked to distinguish between an optimist and .a pessimist. "An optimist," he replied, "is the man who looks after your eyes, and a pessimist is the man who looks after your feet." In advocating the expansion of the Dominion archives, I only wish to go to the bottom of the matter and insist upon the need of laying a solid foundation. Special studies, based on a first hand knowledge of the sources, are the solid pedestal upon which the work of art—the great national history—must stand. Were this the place to discuss details much might be said regarding the organization of a Records Office and the work that might properly be taken up in Canada by a Historical Manuscripts Commission. A single word, perhaps, may be said concerning the materials for local history. These must be looked to with particular care because they are so perishable. Already it is difficult—and often impossible—to make up files of local newspapers from the beginning; and domestic correspondence, even where most valuable—as among the members of leading families—tends to disappear after a generation or so. To take the part of Canada with which I am most familiar, I may say that materials for a minute study of the colonization movement in the Eastern Townships are fast disappearing where already they have not perished. The conditions that prevailed in this country 75 years ago are, generally speaking, so familiar to us that we attach little importance to local records. But two centuries hence the conditions will have changed altogether. Indeed the proper custody of historical materials is among the chief duties which each age owes to its successors.

The sum and substance of what I have sought to urge can be condensed into a very few words. Those who love their country most are often those who are most alive to the contrast between their ideal and actual conditions. When it comes to the subject of history which is close to the heart of every patriot, we would seem to follow the reasonable course in avoiding tall talk and devoting closer attention than heretofore to the systematic study of our own annals.

The subject assumes all the more importance at a time like this, when Canada is making greater progress in things material than ever before; when she is bound up so closely with the international relations of two great powers like Great Britain and the United States; when imperial aspirations are enlarging the political horizon; and when a spirit of hope is abroad on every hand. It is quite clear that, in both volume and scale the interests of Canada will be much greater in the future than they have been in the past. But everything- which makes us look forward with the more confidence should make us look backward with the more sympathy, affection and filial piety.

Appendix III

MEMO BY MR. JOSEPH-EDMOND ROY OF LÉVIS, SECRETARY OF THE CHAMPLAIN SOCIETY, INCLUDED IN A LETTER BY EDMUND WALKER AND A MEMORANDUM BY PROFESSOR GEORGE WRONG TO SIR WILFRID LAURIER, WITH A REQUEST FOR FINANCIAL SUPPORT FOR A PROPOSED EDITION OF CHAMPLAIN'S *WORKS*.

NOVEMBER 21, 1907.[1]

The following is to be included in the Champlain Society edition of Champlain's *Works*:
1. Biographical sketch (translated) of Champlain including the latest researches.
2. Bibliography of the various editions and translations of Champlain's works with critical notes.
3. Notes on the cartography in the works of Champlain.
4. Bibliography of the various works relating to Champlain including the various reviews and critical notes.
5. Notes on the authenticity of the portrait of Champlain.
6. Biography and sketch of Madame de Champlain.
7. Article on Brouage, study of the question of Champlain's grave and enquiry as to the rank of Champlain; was of noble family or not?

Other matters:
1. The text should be carefully compared with each edition, and the different readings should be indicated.
2. There will be explanatory notes of all names and places. The name of the place or of a person mentioned in the text should [not] be passed without a complete explanatory note.
3. Every place pointed out by Champlain should be located and its position and modern name given.
4. The various routes followed by Champlain should be indicated on modern maps.
5. The original maps, drawings of plants, etc., should be reproduced.
6. In an appendix should be collected all the records and documents preserved in the archives both France and England referring to Champlain, to his negotiations, to his travels and to his relations with the Company of One Hundred Associates and with Richelieu.
7. There should be a study of the natural history in his writings and a discussion as to whether he contributed to the work of Cornut.[2]

---

1   MS Coll. 50, Box 48, fol. 1.
2   This appears to be a reference to the writings of the Paris physician and botanist Jacques-Phillippe Cornut who published the following book:
    Cornuti, Iac, *Canadensium plantarum aliarumque nondum editarum Historia Cui adiectum est ad calcem Enchiridion Botanicum Parisiense, Continens Indicem Plantarum, quae in Pagis, Silvis, Pratis, & Montosis iuxta Parisios locis nascuntur.* Parisiis: Venundantur apud Simonem Le Moyne, 1635, 238 pages. Reprinted: (New York: Johnson Reprint Corp., 1966).

8. A reprint at the foot of the pages of the passages in the works of Lescarbot and Sagard which deal with the same subjects as Champlain.
9. A study of the relations between Champlain, the Jesuits and the Recollet.
10. A discussion of the delay caused in the cession back to France of Canada after it's taking by the Kirkes.
11. In an appendix should be inserted a notice of the celebrations of the Champlain Tercentenary at Quebec, St. John, New Brunswick, Annapolis and Champlain, New York.
12. Perhaps it would be well to include illustrations of the various monuments erected to Champlain, views of Brouage, fac-simile of his handwriting, his various portraits, portraits of Madame de Champlain, Richelieu, Henri IV, Henri de Levis, Duke of Ventadour, Duke of Buckingham, negotiator of the peace, etc.

For a discussion of Cornut see: Victoria Dickinson. *Drawn From Life: Science and Art in the Portrayal of the New World* (Toronto: University of Toronto Press, 1998) pp. 78-81. James S. Pringle. "How 'Canadian' is Cornut's Canadensium Plantarum Historia? A Phytogeographic and Historical Analysis." *Canadian Horticultural History,* 1-4 (1988); 190-209.

Appendix IV

Champlain's Original Works, Reprints and Translations

A. Champlain's Original Works

[**n.d.**] "Brief Discours Des choses plus remarquables que Sammuel Champlain De Brouage à Reconneues àux Indes Occidentalles…en Lannee mil vc.iiij.xx [xix] et en Lannee mil vjc.j." Manuscript in John Carter Brown Library, Providence, Rhode Island, Codex Fr. 1 [F], pp. 46, and 62 illustrations.

Note: There are two other manuscript versions of the "Brief Discours," one in Bologna (74 ms pages and 52 illustrations) the other in Turin (55 ms pages and 53 illustrations). It is certain that all three are imperfect copies of an unknown original. It is not known who wrote the three manuscripts or if Champlain wrote the original.

[**n.d.**] *Des Savvages, Ov, Voyage De Samvel Champlain, De Brovage, fait en la France nouuelle, l'an mil six cens trois*: A Paris, Chez Clavde De Monstr'œil, tenant sa boutique en la Cour du Palais, au nom de Iesus.

Privilege: November 15, 1603.

Reprinted: Claude De Monstr'œil in 1604 with slight changes.

Contents: Preliminary material, pp. i–vii. Divided into 13 chapters, pp. 1–36 fol. pages. Length, 76 pages. Events: March 15, 1603 to September 20, 1603.

1613. *Les Voyages Dv Sievr De Champlain Xaintongeois, Capitaine ordinaire pour le Roy, en la marine*. A Paris, Chez Iean Berjon, rue S. Iean de Beauuais, au Cheual volant, & en sa boutique au Palais, à la gallerie des prisonniers. M.DC.XIII.

Privilege: January 9, 1613.

Contents: *Livre Premier. Auquel sont descrites les descouuertures de la coste d'Acadie & de la Floride*. Seventeen chapters, pp.1–160. [Events: March 7, 1604 to September 30, 1607].

Livre Second. Auquel sont descrits les voyages faites au grand fleuue Sainct Laurens, par le sieur de Champlain. Eleven chapters, pp. 161–240.
[Events: April 5, 1608 to February, 1610].

Second Voyage Dv Sieur De Champlain fait en la Nouuelle France en l'annee 1610.
Three chapters, pp. 241–270.
[Events: March 7, 1610 to September 27, 1610].

Le Troisiesme Voyage Dv Sievr De Champlain en l'annee 1611. Four chapters, pp. 271–331. [
[Events: March 1, 1611 to September 10, 1611 to 1612].

| | *Qvatriesme Voyage Dv Sr De Champlain…fait en l,annee 1613.* Five chapters, pp. 3–52. Separate pagination from rest of book. |
| | [Events: Late 1611 to 1612. March 5, 1613 to September 26, 1613]. |

Illustrations:
> Two folding maps; 22 small maps and picture plans.

1619. *Voyages Et Descovvertures Faites En La Novvelle France, depuis l'année 1615. iusques à la fin de l'année 1618…* A Paris, Chez Clavde Collet, au Palais, en la gallerie des Prisonniers. M.D.C.XIX.

Privilege: May 18, 1619.

Reprinted: Claude Collet with some changes in 1620 and 1627.

Contents: Preliminary material, pp. i–xvi. No chapters, pp. 1–158 fol. pages.
[Events: February 28, 1615 to August 28, 1616].

Illustrations:
> Five pictures one map. One large incomplete map dated 1616 intended for, but not published in the book.

1632. *Les Voyages De La Novvelle France Occidentale, Dicte Canada,…* A Paris, Chez Clavde Collet au Palais, en la Gallerie des Prisonniers, à l'Estoille d'Or. M.DC.XXXII.

Privilege: none.

Simultaneous printings by:
> A Paris, Chez Louis Sevestre Imprimeur-Libraire rue du Meurier prés la Porte S. Victor, & en sa Boutique dans la Cour du Palais, M.DC.XXXII.
>
> A Paris, Chez Pierre Le-Mvr, dans la grand' Salle du Palais. M.DC.XXXII.

Reprinted: with some changes in 1640 by Collet and Le-Mur.

Contents: Preliminary material, pp. 1–8.

La Premier Partie:

Livre Premier. Eight chapters, pp. 1–48. Events: Early exploration to end of 1603].

Livre Second. Eight chapters, pp. 49–97. Events: early 1604 to end of 1607.

Livre Troisieme. Fourteen chapters, pp. 98–181. Events: about 1607 to August 11, 1611.

Livre Qvatriesme. Eight chapters, pp. 182–229. Events: March 5, 1613 to May 7, 1620.

La Seconde Partie:

Livre Premier. Eight chapters, pp. 1–78. Events: June 1620 to April 1625.

Livre Second. Six chapters, pp. 79–184. Events: February 1625 to late May, 1629.

Lievre Troisieme. Seven chapters, pp. 185–310. Events: May 20, 1629 to early 1632.

Table Pour Cognoistre Les Lieux Remarquables En Ceste Carte. Pages 1–8.

Table Des Chapitres. Pages 9–16.

>
> *Traitté De La Marine....* Pp. 1–54.
>
> *Doctrine Chrestienne...Traduicte en Langage Canadois...Par le R. P. Brebœuf....*
> Pages 1–15.
>
> *L'Oraison Dominicale Traduite En Langage Des Montagnar...Par le R. P. Massé....*
> Pages 16–20.

Illustrations:
> Nine illustrations, six the same as in 1619 volume; one large folding map dated 1632.

B. Reprints and Translations

1625. Samuel de Champlain, "The Voyage of Samuel Champlaine of Brouage, made unto Canada in the yeere 1603, dedicated to Charles de Montmorencie, &c. High Admirall of France," in *Hakluytus Posthumus or Purchas His Pilgrimes. Contayning a History of the World, in Sea voyages & lande Travells, by Englishmen & others,* comp. Samuel Purchas (London: Printed by William Stansby for Henrie Featherstone, and are to be sold at his shop in Pauls Church-yard at the signe of the Rose), The Fourth Part, Book VIII, chap. VI: 1605–1619.

Note: First English translation, probably by Richard Hakluyt, of any of Champlain's writings.

1830. Samuel de Champlain, *Voyages du Sieur de Champlain, ou, Journal ès découvertes de la Nouvelle France,* 2 vols, (Paris: Imprimé aux frais du gouvernment pou procurer du travail aux ouvriers typographes).

Note: A reprint of *Les Voyages...1632,* without the *Traitte De La Marine* or any of the other supplementary material.

1859. Samuel de Champlain, *Narrative of a voyage to the West Indies and Mexico in the years 1599–1602,* ed. Norton Shaw, trans. Alice Wilmere (London: The Hakluyut Society).

Note: This is the first translation and printing of *Brief discours*, a manuscript of Champlain's West Indian voyage attributed to Champlain.

1870. Samuel de Champlain, *Œuvres de Champlain publiés sous le patronage de l'Université Laval,* 6 vols, 2nd edition, ed. Charles-Honoré Laverdière (Québec: Imprimé au Séminaire par Geo.-E. Desbarats).

Reprinted: Montréal: Editions du Jour, 1973.

Note: This is the first collation of all of Champlain's books and a number of contemporary documents.

1880. Samuel de Champlain, *Voyages of Samuel De Champlain,* 3 vols, ed. Edmund Slafter, trans. Charles Pomeroy Otis (Boston: The Prince Society).

Reprinted: edited by William L. Grant (New York: Charles Scribner's Sons, 1907).

Reprinted: New York: Burt Franklin, 1966–67.

Note: Translation of *Des Sauvages*...[n.d.] collated with the printing of 1604; *Les Voyages...1613*; and *Voyages Et Descouvertures...1619*. The reprint of 1907 omits *Des Sauvages*.

1906. Samuel de Champlain, *The Voyages and Explorations of Samuel de Champlain (1604–1616) Narrated by Himself...Together with the Voyage of 1603 Reprinted from Purchas His Pilgrimes*, 2 vols, ed. Edward Gaylord Bourne, trans. Annie Nettleton Bourne (New York: A.S. Barnes).

Reprinted: edited by William L. Grant (Toronto: Courier Press, 1911).

Reprinted: New York: Allerton Book Co., 1922

Reprinted: New York: AMS Press, 1977.

Reprinted: Dartmouth, NS: Brook House Press, 2000.

Note: Translation of the first four books of *Les Voyages...1632*, and a reprint of the Purchas translation of 1625.

1922–36. Samuel de Champlain, *The Works of Samuel De Champlain reprinted, translated and annotated by six Canadian scholars under the general editorship of H.P. Biggar*, 6 vols, gen. ed. Henry P. Biggar, (Toronto: The Champlain Society).

Reprinted Toronto: University of Toronto Press, 1971.

Note: A careful collation of all of Champlain's printed texts, as well as some documents, translated into English.

1951. Samuel de Champlain, *Les voyages de Samuel de Champlain, saintongeais, père du Canada*, ed. Hubert Jules Deschamps, (Paris: Presses universitaires de France).

Note: Volume contains: *Brief Discours, Des Sauvages, Les Voyages 1613, Voyages Et Descouvertures, 1619* and four chapters (1627–29) from *Les Voyages, 1632*.

1966. Samuel de Champlain, *Les Voyages Dv Sievr De Champlain Xaintongeois, Capitaine ordinaire pour le Roy, en la marine*. A Paris, Chez Iean Berjon, rue S. Iean de Beauuais, au Cheual volant, & en sa boutique au Palais, à la gallerie des prisonniers. M.DC.XIII. (Ann Arbour: Facsimile Reprint by University Microfilms, Inc).

1971. Samuel de Champlain, *Voyages to New France. Being a narrative of the many remarkable things...1599 to 1601, with an account...in the year 1603*, trans. Michael Macklem, intro. Edward Miles (Ottawa: Oberon)
 Samuel de Champlain, *Voyages to New France. Being an Account...1615–1618*, transl. Michael Macklem, intro. Edward Miles (Ottawa: Oberon).

Note: The first volume is a very free translation of *Brief Discours* and *Des Sauvages*. It contains the errors of the 1625 Purchas translation and all Champlain's leagues are converted to miles by multiplying them by three. The second volume is a free translation of *Voyages Et Descovvertures, 1619*.

1978. Samuel de Champlain, *Des Sauvages: a facsimile of the Paris, 1603, edition, made from the copy at the John Carter Brown Library, Brown University, Providence Rhode Island; with an introduction by Marcel Trudel,* (Montréal: Designed at The Stinehour Press, printed at The Meriden Gravure Co. for G. Javitch).

1993. Samuel de Champlain. *Des Sauvages. Texte établi, présenté et annoté par Alain Beaulieu et Réal Ouellet,* (Montréal: Éditions Typo).

1994. Samuel de Champlain, *La France d'Amérique: Voyages de Samuel Champlain, 1604–1629,* intro. Jean Glénisson (Paris: Imprimerie nationale).

Note: A reprint of Champlain's voyages from 1604 to 1629.

Appendix V

LETTER: HENRY PERCIVAL BIGGAR TO GEORGE WRONG, APRIL 15, 1911.

15th April, 1911.
34, Oxford Mansion, W.

My dear Mr. Wrong,

Many thanks for your letters of 6 January and 6 March, which I should have acknowledged sooner, but was waiting for Mr. Langton's translations of Laverdière I and II. These have now come and I have read them through. They are very satisfactory and Mr. Langton deserves much credit for his labours. Will you have a cheque for $100 paid to him please for his translation, of Champlain's "Voyage to the West Indies" and of the "Voyage to the St. Lawrence" in 1603?[3]

It is my intention to go over his translations with the French text, and should any alteration or corrections suggest themselves I shall add these in lead pencil. I shall then return his MSS. to hear what observations he may like to make on my corrections. His notes are somewhat verbose, and he has not always followed the punctuation of the original. When his MSS. come back they will practically be ready for the printer. As no news has come about Winship's work, I am writing to him to let me have the results of his labours.[4] Since reading Mr, Langton's translation of the "Voyage to the West Indies" I have come to the conclusion that the plates are scattered through the original MSS. and do not come altogether at the end as reproduced in Laverdière volume I. If this be the case we must reproduce them in their proper order in the volume. Otherwise the text does not read well.

If Winship has collated volumes I and II of Laverdière's text with the original there is very little for Roy to do but to run through Laverdière's notes.[5] We should I think restrict the notes of the French text merely to the identification of the places mentioned, otherwise the same long note would be repeated in English and in French. We are having very full notes, to the translation and can refer readers of the French text to these. I am writing to Roy to this effect, asking him to begin at once to collate pages 1 to 133 of the 1613 edition of Champlain. This is Livre I of Laverdière's volume III, which must be included in our first volume. Ganong wrote me, he had his translation of this section well in hand, and I am asking him to send it to me at the end of May, by which date I hope to return Mr. Langton's MSS. for his observation on my corrections. On examining again in the light of your letters of 7 April 1909 and 21 October 1910, the question of the number of volumes to be issued I find there will have to be six, exclusive of that which is to contain Champlain's life and the documents relating to his career.

My first suggestion that we should publish a volume (No.1) with only Laverdière's volumes I and II, I find is not feasible. This would only make 60,000 words or some 170 pages. The section

---

3   The book referred to is *Des Sauvages*.
4   George Parker Winship of the John Carter Brown Library at Providence, R.I., was asked to proof read the French text against the originals at that library.
5   Joseph-Edmond Roy was had just been appointed Head of the new manuscript division of the archives in Ottawa. Biggar had asked him to collate the French texts.

of Laverdière volume III which Ganong is doing will make this volume (including the 64 plates of Laverdiere volume I) up to about 400 pages.

Our second volume will then consist, of the remainder of the 1613 edition of Champlain (Laverdiere volume III pages l35-326). Grant was to revise his translation of this section for us, but in view of the delay in his translation of Lescarbot, of his work at Queen's and of his marriage, I would suggest we ask Col. Wood of Quebec, to translate this volume. This section deals with the foundation of Quebec and it would be well to have it done by a man thoroughly conversant with the ground. You mentioned his name to me and stated he was a good French scholar. I am writing to ask him if he will do this volume for us.

Roy is to revise both Laverdière's text and notes for this volume. I shall ask him if he has done anything in this matter when I write him about his notes to our first volume.

Our third volume will contain the whole of Laverdière's volume IV (which is the 1619 edition of Champlain) and also the first 126 pages of Laverdière's volume V. This latter is simply a repetition of the first portion of the 1613 Champlain which Ganong is translating, and if Ganong's work is satisfactory I shall ask him to do these 126 pages as well. Grant was to do Laverdière's volume IV for this third volume, but in view of what I have stated above, I think we should ask Mr. Langton to translate it for us. If you think my suggestion a good one and Mr. Langton will undertake this for $135 he might begin at once. He will find translations of this work in volume III of the Prince Society's edition pp 89 to 218, and In Grant's volume on Champlain in the series of Original Narratives of Early American History pp 263-361, edited by Jameson. Our fourth volume will consist of the remaining portion of Laverdière's volume V (pp 127-328). If Grant will undertake this, well and good. If not, however, and Wood accepts the offer to translate pp 136-326 of Laverdière's volume III for our second volume, and his work is satisfactory, I shall ask him to translate as well these pages 127-328 of Laverdière's volume V for our fourth volume. This covers for the most part the same ground as the latter portion of the 1613 Champlain, which as stated above, I propose to ask Col. Wood to translate. With regard to Laverdière's volume VI which Mr. Le Sueur has translated, I find it too bulky to be published in one volume when the French text is to be printed in large type. I suggest, therefore, we publish it in two volumes, our fifth volume ending at page 206. Our sixth volume would then contain the remainder of Laverdière's volume VI. I have not yet chosen a translator for the Traité de la Marine, but shall do so as soon as I have seen Mr. Le. Sueur's translation. I understand he has sent this to you and shall be glad to hear how you find it. If it is decided to publish a life of Champlain this should form our seventh volume which would also contain the original text and translations of all the documents relating to his career.

Grant seemed to think he would be able to do a life for us later on and I intend to ask him to do so when he comes over next month. You have my authority for the payment on account of $100 to Mr. Le Sueur for his translation of Laverdière's volume VI. With regard to this matter of remuneration, I understand from your letter of 9 April 1909, that I am to be paid $500 for each volume we issue, out of which is to come the payments to the translators and sub-editors. This new arrangement supersedes I suppose the old agreement that I was to receive $1,000 for my services? I certainly think, as I am to revise all the translations and also the notes of the French text that I should be paid at least $200 a volume. For instance, in the case of volume I, the payments would be $100 to Mr. Langton, $50 to Mr. Winship, $50 to Roy, and $65 to Ganong. This would leave $235 out of which I should take $200. In this connection there will also be the cost of the reproduction of the plates of the original MSS. of Champlain's "Voyage to the West Indies". Four of these Nos. LVII, LIX. LX, and LXI, are coloured and should be reproduced in colours. I understand the cost of reproducing these plates as well as all the maps will be paid for separately. Will you kindly let me know definitely in regard to these monetary matters so that there will be no confusion or misunderstanding later on?

As the Society is unable to pay me for the second volume of Lescarbot, may I make bold to ask for a payment of £50 on account for my work in connection with this edition of Champlain? This will include the revision of all the translations and notes as well as a careful scrutiny of the French text and notes. Should Grant be willing to write the life of Champlain I would supply him with copies of all the documents to be found in the French archives bearing on Champlain's career.

Please give my kindest regards to Mrs Blake and Mrs. Wrong. Sammy and his wife are in Torquay and must be having glorious weather for it is delightful even here in London. Hoping to see you over here before long and that you will let me have a reply to this letter shortly,

Yours sincerely,
Henry P. Biggar

Appendix VI

The National Battlefields Commission
71 Peter Street

Sir George Garneau, Chairman
Lucien Pacaud, Secretary

Quebec September 29 1938.

Mr. W. S. Wallace, M.A., F.R.S.C.,
The Library,
University of Toronto,
Toronto.

My dear Mr. Wallace,

I have your letter of the 26th instant with reference to the undertaking, by the Champlain Society, of the publication of a popular edition of the Works of Samuel Champlain.

I have examined the records of the Commission in this connection, and I do not find in the resolutions consigned, in its minutes any formal undertaking or conditions to this effect. I have a clear remembrance that this was mooted at the time by Sir Edmund Walker and professor Wrong, but no formal resolution to this effect was ever passed.

I quite agree with you that the publication of such a popular edition would entail a heavy loss to the Champlain Society, as no doubt the sale of this edition would be very limited at this late date.

Under these circumstances I will advise my colleagues at the next meeting of the Commission to relieve your Society of any obligation in this respect. Meanwhile the matter may rest in peace, as it has done for thirty years.

Yours sincerely
J. Geo. Garneau
Chairman N.B.C.

TABLES

TABLE 1 Relationship between the Laverdière edition and the Champlain Society edition

Volume	Laverdière edition	Champlain Society edition
1	Brief Discours. [n.d.] – pp. 110.	Brief Discours, [n.d.] Des Sauvages, [n.d.], 1604. Les Voyages, 1613–to end of Livre Premier.
2	Des Sauvages. [n.d.] – pp. 55.	Les Voyages, 1613–Livre Second to end of book.
3	Les Voyages, 1613. - pp. 354.	Voyages Et Descouvertures, 1619, 1620, 1627. Les Voyages, 1632–Premier Partie to end of Livre Second.
4	Voyages Et Descouvertures, 1619. – pp. 150.	Les Voyages, 1632–Premier Partie to end of Livre Quatriesme.
5	Les Voyages, 1632, to end of Premier Partie.–pp. 328.	Les Voyages, 1632–Second Partie to end of Livre Second.
6	Les Voyages, 1632, Second Partie to end of book, and contemporary documents. – pp. 442.	Les Voyages, 1632–Livre Troisieme to end of book.

Note: For complete bibliographic entries and listing of Champlain's original publications, see Appendix IV. Laverdière examined handwritten transcriptions of *Brief Discours* and *Des Sauvages*. It is not known how many printings of *Les Voyages*, 1613, *Voyages Et Descouvertures*, 1619, 1620, 1627, and *Les Voyages*, 1632, he collated. Eventually the Champlain Society editor J. Home Cameron, collated three copies of *Des Sauvages* (n.d.) with one copy of the 1604 printing and an unknown number of copies of *Les Voyages, 1613*. He collated nine copies of *Voyages Et Descouvertures,* 1619 and 1620 with five of the 1627 printing. Cameron examined twenty-two copies of *Les Voyages, 1632* printed by Le-Mur, Sevestre and Collet, and four copies of the 1640 reprint by Le-Mur and Collet. Of these he collated eight of the 1632 printing with three printed in 1640. Both editors used only the manuscript of *Brief Discours* in the John Carter Brown Library. The page numbers given for the length of the Laverdière volumes cover only the length of the Champlain texts that were reproduced and do not include the introductory material.

TABLE 2 A Publication accepted, in progress, printed and cancelled, 1906–1910

Editor(s)	Short Title	1906	1907	1908	1909	1910
Grant/Biggar	Lescarbot: History vol. 1	0	1			
Grant/Biggar	Lescarbot: History vol. 2	0	=	=	=	=
Grant/Biggar	Lescarbot: History vol. 3	0	=	=	=	=
Ganong	Denys: Description and Natural	0	=	2		
Munro	Seigniorial Documents	0	=	=	3	
Shortt	Cartwright Papers	0	=	=	=	=
Wood	Logs of the Conquest of Canada	0	=	=	=	4
McLennan	Louisbourg	0	=	=	=	=
Tyrrell	Hearne Journal		0	=	=	=
Doughty/Wrong	Knox Journals vol. 1		0	=	=	=
Doughty/Wrong	Knox Journals vol. 2		0	=	=	=
Doughty/Wrong	Knox journals vol. 3		0	=	=	=
Burpee/Le Sueur	La Vérendrye Journals		0	=	=	=
Biggar et.al.	Champlain's Works vol. 1		0	=	=	=
Biggar et.al.	Champlain's Works vol. 2		0	=	=	=
Biggar et.al.	Champlain's Works vol. 3		0	=	=	=
Biggar et.al.	Champlain's Works vol. 4		0	=	=	=
Biggar et.al.	Champlain's Works vol. 5		0	=	=	=
Biggar et.al.	Champlain's Works vol. 6		0	=	=	=
Ganong	Le Clercq Relation			0	=	5
Roy	Rebellion of 1837			0	=	X
McArthur/Doughty	General Murray's Régime				0	=
Wood	War of 1812 ("Wood's War") vol. 1					0
Wood	War of 1812 vol. 2					0
Wood	War of 1812 vol. 3					0
Wood	War of 1812 vol. 4					0

Source: MS Coll 50, item 66, Minute Book, 1905–25.
Note: Accepted for publication: 0; Editing in progress: =; Year printed and publication number, i.e.: 18; Publication cancelled: X; *Champlain's Works* were un-numbered, i.e.: Un 3.

TABLE 2 B Publications accepted, in progress, printed and cancelled, 1911–1922

Editor(s)	Short Title	1911	1912	1913	1914	1915	1916	1917	1918	1919	1920	1921	1922
Grant/Biggar	Lescarbot: History v. 2	7											
Grant/Biggar	Lescarbot: History v. 3	=	=	=	11								
Shortt	Cartwright Papers	=	=	X									
McLennan	Louisbourg	=	=	X									
Tyrrell	Hearne Journal	6											
Doughty/Wrong	Knox Journals v. 1	=	=	=	8								
Doughty/Wrong	Knox Journals v. 2	=	=	=	=	9							
Doughty/Wrong	Knox Journals v. 3	=	=	=	=	=	10						
Burpee/Le Sueur	La Vérendrye Journals	=	=	=	=	=	=	=	=	=	=	=	=
Biggar et al.	Champlain's Works v. 1	=	=	=	=	=	=	=	=	=	=	=	=
Biggar et al.	Champlain's Works v. 2	=	=	=	=	=	=	=	=	=	=	=	Un 1
Biggar et al.	Champlain's Works v. 3	=	=	=	=	=	=	=	=	=	=	=	=
Biggar et al.	Champlain's Works v. 4	=	=	=	=	=	=	=	=	=	=	=	=
Biggar et al.	Champlain's Works v. 5	=	=	=	=	=	=	=	=	=	=	=	=
Biggar et al.	Champlain's Works v. 6	=	=	=	=	=	=	=	=	=	=	=	=
McArthur/Doughty	General Murray's Régime	=	=	=	=	=	=	=	=	X	13		
Wood	War of 1812 ("Wood's War") v. 1	=	=	=	=	=	=	=	=	=	=	=	
Wood	War of 1812 ("Wood's War") v. 2	=	=	=	=	=	=	=	=	=	=	=	=
Wood	War of 1812 ("Wood's War") v. 3	=	=	=	=	=	=	=	=	=	=	=	=
Wood	War of 1812 ("Wood's War") v. 4	=	=	=	=	=	=	=	=	=	=	=	=

(Table 2 b continued on next page)

(Table 2 b continued from previous page)

Editor(s)	Short Title	1911	1912	1913	1914	1915	1916	1917	1918	1919	1920	1921	1922
Webster/Ganong	Diérville: Port Royal	0	=	=	=	=	=	=	=	=	=	=	=
Tyrrell	Thompson's Narrative		0	=	=	=	=	12					
Kylie	Bagot's Administration		0	=	=	X							
Grant/Laycock	Clergy Reserves		0	=	=	X							
Burpee	R.. Campbell's Journals			0	X								
Melville	Petitot's Explorations				0	=	=	=	=	X			

Source: MS Coll 50, item 66, Minute Book, 1905–25.

Note: Accepted for publication: 0; Editing in progress: =; Year printed and publication number, i.e.: 18; Publication cancelled: X; Champlain's Works were un-numbered, i.e.: Un 3.

TABLE 2 C Publications accepted, in progress, printed and cancelled, 1923–1937

Editor(s)	Short Title	1923	1924	1925	1926	1927	1928	1929	1930	1931	1932	1933	1934	1935	1936	1937
Burpee	La Vérendrye Journals	=	=	=	=	16										
Biggar et.al.	Champlain's Works v. 2	=	=	Un 2												
Biggar et.al.	Champlain's Works v. 3	=	=	=	=	=	=	Un 3								
Biggar et.al	Champlain's Works v. 4	=	=	=	=	=	=	=	=	=	Un 4					
Biggar et.all.	Champlain's Works v. 5	=	=	=	=	=	=	=	=	=	=	Un 5				
Biggar et.al.	Champlain's Works v. 6	=	=	=	=	=	=	=	=	=	=	=	=	=	Un 6	
Wood	War of 1812 v. 2	14														
Wood	War of 1812 v. 3	=	=	=	=	15										
Wood	War of 1812 v. 4	=	=	=	=	=	17									
Webster	Diérville: Port Royal	=	=	=	=	=	=	=	=	=	=	20				
Wallace	North West Co. Docs.	=	=	=	=	=	=	=	=	=	=	=	22			
Doughty	Elgin/Grey Papers		0	X												
Wallace/Tyrrell	Early Hist. / Hudson Bay					0	=	=	=	18						
Johnson	Vancouver's Voyages								0	=	=	=	X			
Robinson	Du Creux: Historia v. 1									0	=	=	=	=	=	=
Robinson	Du Creux: Historia v. 2									0	=	=	=	=	=	=
Wallace	McLean's Notes									0	19					
Tyrrell	Hearne and Turnor									0	=	=	21			
Wrong/Langton	Sagard: Grand Voyage										0	=	=	=	=	=

(Table 2 c continued on next page)

(Table 2 c continued from previous page)

Editor(s)	Short Title	1923	1924	1925	1926	1927	1928	1929	1930	1931	1932	1933	1934	1935	1936	1937
Burpee/Jenness	Simon Fraser										0	=	=	=	=	X
Morton	Ross: Peace River										0	X				
Seton	Hutchins: Natural Hist.										0	X				
Langton	Patrick Campbell												0	=	=	23
Nute	Radisson and Groseilliers												0	X		
Glazebrook	Hargrave, 1821-43												0	=	=	=

Source: MS Coll 50, item 66, Minute Book, 1905–25; item 67, Minute book, 1926–48.

Note: Accepted for publication 0; Editing in progress =; Year printed and publication number, i.e. 18; Publication cancelled X; *Champlain's Works* were unnumbered, i.e. Un 3.

TABLE 2 D Publications accepted, in progress, printed and cancelled, 1938–1949

Editor(s)	Short Title	1938	1939	1940	1941	1942	1943	1944	1945	1946	1947	1948	1949
Robinson	*Du Creux: Historia v. 1*	=	=	=	=	=	=	=	=	=	=	=	=
Robinson	*Du Creux: Historia v. 2*	=	=	=	=	=	=	=	=	=	=	=	=
Glazebrook	*Hargrave, 1821–43*	24											
Rich	*Simpson Athabasca*	HB1											
Wrong/Langton	*Sagard: Grand Voyage*	=	25										
Brown	*La Terrière Mémoires*	0	X										
Rich	*Robertson Letters, 1817–22*	0	HB2										
Fauteux	*Montcalm Letters*		0	X									
Fauteux	*Baby Collection*		0	X									
Blair	*Perrot's Memoires*		0	X									
Howay	*Colnett Journal*	0	=	26									
Talman	*Loyalist Narratives*	0	0	=	=	=	=	=	=	27			
Fleming	*Northern Dept. 1821–31*	0	=	HB3									
Rich	*McLoughlin, Vanc. 1825–28*			0	HB4								
Rich	*McLoughlin, Vanc. 1839–44*			0	=	=	HB6						
Rich	*McLoughlin, Vanc. 1844–46*			0	=	=	=	HB7					
Rich	*Minutes, HBC, 1671–74*				0	HB5							
Rich	*Minutes, HBC, 1679–82*							0	HB8				
Rich	*Minutes, HBC, 1682–84*							0	=	HB9			
Rich	*Despatch, Simpson*									0	HB10		

(Table 2 d continued on next page)

(Table 2 d continued from previous page)

Editor(s)	Short Title	1938	1939	1940	1941	1942	1943	1944	1945	1946	1947	1948	1949
MacLeod	*Letitia Hargrave*					0	=	=	=	=	28		
Rich	*Letters Out. 1680–87*										0	HB11	
Innis	*Simeon Perkins v. 1*								0	=	=	29	
Rich	*Isham's Observations, 1743*											0	HB12

Source: MS Coll 50, item 66, Minute Book, 1905–25; item 67, Minute book, 1926–48.

Note: Accepted for publication 0; Editing in progress =; Year printed and publication number, i.e. 24; Publication cancelled X; Hudson Bay Company Series (1938–49) was numbered separately, i.e. HB1.

TABLE 3 A Costs of Champlain Society Volumes, 1907-1937

Vol.	Date	Editor(s)	Short Title	Print. Cost $	Tot. Costs $
1	1907	Grant/Biggar	Lescarbot: History v. 1	831.98	1568.05
2	1908	Ganong	Denys: Description and Natural	1264.17	2029.09
3	1908	Munro	Seigniorial Documents	844.93	1450.74
4	1909	Wood	Logs of the Conquest of Canada	651.77	1806.19
5	1910	Ganong	Le Clercq Relation	891.77	1649.70
6	1911	Tyrrell	Hearne Journal	1251.32	2061.70
7	1911	Grant/Biggar	Lescarbot: History v. 2	1118.45	2234.03
8	1914	Doughty/Wrong	Knox Journals v. 1	1271.12	2418.66
9	1915	Doughty/Wrong	Knox Journals v. 2	1538.69	2437.59
10	1916	Doughty/Wrong	Knox Journals v. 3	1667.74	2688.08
11	1914	Grant/Biggar	Lescarbot: History v. 3	1152.27	2053.21
12	1917	Tyrrell	Thompson's Narrative	1955.17	2451.23
13	1920	Wood	War of 1812 ("Wood's War") v. 1	1152.26	2803.87
Un 1	1922	Biggar et.al.	Champlain's Works v. 1	5151.78	8240.76
14	1923	Wood	War of 1812 v. 2	2510.86	2803.87
Un 2	1925	Biggar et.al.	Champlain's Works v. 2	3044.09	3933.28
15	1926	Wood	War of 1812 v. 3	2387.82	2803.87
16	1927	Burpee	La Vérendrye Journals	3008.73	3563.98
17	1928	Wood	War of 1812 v. 4	2402.09	2803.87
Un 3	1929	Biggar et.al.	Champlain's Works v. 3	2705.14	3490.14
18	1931	Wallace/Tyrrell	Early Hist. Hudson Bay	2421.67	2673.67
Un 4	1932	Biggar et.al.	Champlain's Works v. 4	1916.70	2703.22
19	1932	Wallace	McLean's Notes	1483.88	2090.07
Un 5	1933	Biggar et.al.	Champlain's Works v. 5	1988.28	2588.29
20	1933	Webster	Dièrville: Port Royal	1735.49	2255.49
21	1934	Tyrrell	Hearne and Turnor	3652.23	4495.60
22	1934	Wallace	North West Company	2267.83	2919.93
Un 6	1936	Biggar et.al.	Champlain's Works v. 6	2462.92	3562.92
23	1937	Langton	Patrick Campbell	1094.71	1996.01

Source: Data obtained from: MS Coll. 50, item 15, General Ledger, 1906–1962, and box 18, fol., 35, "Analysis of costs of Books." The ledger and other accounting data are difficult to interpret. In the case of some volumes dollar figures are given without explanation what that includes, in other cases a detailed costing is given. Wherever possible only costs directly related to the editing and production of a book have been included in this table. General office outlays were not included. The material in box 18 is a detailed analysis of the cost of the first twelve volumes. All figures are in Canadian currency.

Notes: Column one: Volume numbers are those assigned by The Champlain Society. *Champlain's Works* were designated an unnumbered series in 1920.
–The final cost of each volume of the *War of 1812* by Colonel Wood is impossible to calculate. An average was derived from the total cost of the four volumes.
–Volume 18, *Documents Relating to the Early History of Hudson Bay*, edited by Wallace and Tyrrell, was the first volume published in Canada by the University of Toronto Press. Ballantyne Press and its successor Spottiswoode, Ballantyne & Co. of London, England, published all previous volumes and all volumes of *Champlain's Works*. Maclehose Press, Glasgow, published the Hudson's Bay Series between 1938 and 1949.

TABLE 3 B Costs of Champlain Society Volumes, 1938-1948

Vol.	Date	Editor(s)	Short Title	Printing Cost $	Total Cost $
24	1938	Glazebrook	Hargrave, 1821-43	2139.26	3948.77
HB1	1938	Rich/Martin	Sinpson Athabasca	2102.68	2602.68
25	1939	Wrong/Langton	Sagard: Grand Voyage	2182.68	2706.38
HB2	1939	Rich	Robertson Letters, 1817-22	2058.14	2558.14
26	1940	Howay	Colnett Journal	2437.98	3546.40
HB3	1940	Fleming/Innis	Northern Dept, 1821-31	2138.51	2638.51
HB4	1941	Rich/Lamb	McLoughlin, Vanc. 1825-28	2000.55	2708.44
HB5	1942	Rich/Clapham	Minutes, HBC, 1671-74	2049.69	2549.65
HB6	1943	Rich/Lamb	McLoughlin, Vanc. 1839-44	2009.05	2509.05
HB7	1944	Rich/Lamb	McLoughlin, Vanc. 1844-46	2000.07	2500.07
HB8	1945	Rich/Clark	Minutes, HBC, 1679-82	2005.01	2505.01
27	1946	Talman	Loyalist Narratives	2012.75	3103.75
HB9	1946	Rich/Clark	Minutes HBC, 1682-84	2005.01	2505.01
28	1947	MacLeod	Letitia Hargrave	4446.08	5081.56
HB10	1947	Rich/Wallace	Despatch, Simpson	2000.00	2500.00
29	1948	Innis	Simeon Perkins v. 1	3471.66	3971.66
HB11	1948	Rich/Taylor	Letters Out. 1680-87	1625.85	2125.85
HB12	1949	Rich/Johnson	Isham's Observations, 1743-49	Gift - HBC	Gift - HBC

Source: Data obtained from: MS Coll. 50, item 15, General Ledger, 1906-1962.
Notes: Column one: Volume numbers are those assigned by The Champlain Society. Hudson's Bay Company Series volumes were numbered separately.
All figures are in Canadian currency.
Total paid for volume 24, *Hargrave Correspondence, 1821–43* includes purchase of the letters for $1269.51.

TABLE 4 Champlain Society financial data, 1905-1939

Date	A	B	C	D	E	F	G	H
1905	1	1 & 2	1907 & 1908	-	-	153	-	-
1906				-	2060	-	1907	
1907				1907	370	600	1677	
1908	2	3 & 4	1909 & 1910	1677	610	1320	967	
1909				967	3261	3426	796	
1910	3	5 & 6	1910 & 1911	796	3311	1588	2519	
1911	4	7 & 8	1911 & 1914	2519	2570	2128	1461	4000[1]
1912				1461	5359[2]	3121	3698	3598
1913	5	9 & 10	1915 & 1916	7296[3]	3322	4468	6150	
1914	6	11 & 12	1914 & 1917	6150	856	2599	4406	
1915				4406	4657	6632	2431	
1916				No data	No data	No data	No data	
1917	7	13	1920	526	5531	5448	608	
1918	8	Un 1	1922	608	1413	1981	40	
1919				40	3370	763	2647	
1920	9	14	1923	2647	1162	344	3465	
1921				3465	3665	No data	No data	
1922	10	Un 2	1925	No data	3356	8824	1663	
1923				1663	5379	5196	1845	
1924				1845	3854	1274	4425	
1925	11	15	1927	4425	3738	7063	1080	2574[4]
1926	12	16	1927	1080	1436	601	1916	2652
1927	13	17	1928	1952	10,644	7374	5316	2732
1928	14	Un 3	1929	5316	5910	3462	7764	2941
1929				7764	1695	8795[5]	634	8330*
1930	15	18	1931	634	7693[6]	4315	4012	7174*
1931	16	Un 4	1932	4012	5040	4399	4653	7661*
1932	17	19 & Un 5	1932 & 1933	4653	5240	5935	3959	7728*
1933	18	20 & 21	1933 & 1934	3959	5160	5380	3738	8222*
1934	19	22 & Un 6	1934 & 1936	3738	7992[7]	8287	3443	481*

(Table 4 continued on next page)

(Table 4 continued from previous page)

Date	A	B	C	D	E	F	G	H
1935	20	23 & 24	1937 & 1938	3443	1205	3300	1348	1095*
1936	21	HB1 & 25	1938 & 1939	1348	5065	5169	1244	1806*
1937				1244	1395	2990	-351	2344*
1938	22	HB2 & 26	1939 & 1940	-351	7574[8]	4226	3320	385*
1939	23	HB3 & 4	1940 & 1941	3320	6070[9]	7498	1892	217*

Sources: MS Coll. 50, items 66 and 67, Minute Books; Ibid., box 18, fol., 9, "Explanation of Fees Paid."
Note: All figures in Canadian currency rounded to the nearest dollar.
Column headings are as follows: A: Invoice number;
B: Invoice per publication number(s) – UN 1 Unnumbered series of Champlain's Works, HB1 Hudson's Bay series;
C: Date publications printed;
D: Balance forward from previous year;
E: Income (fees, interest on accounts and investments, account transfers; back publications;
F: Disbursements;
G: Balance current account;
H: Balance savings account.

1   Savings account created with $2500 from the National Battlefields Commission and $1500 from current account.
2   Includes $500 from savings account.
3   Current and savings accounts were combined and savings account closed.
4   Second instalment of $2500 and interest from National Battlefields Commission to open savings account.
5   To savings account $5000 and $3000 to purchase debentures.
6   From savings account $1650.
7   From savings account $1308.
8   Includes $2500 moved from savings account.
9   Includes $700 moved from investments. * Does not include value of interest-bearing bonds, debentures and other investments. In 1929 these totalled $3000 and 1939, $13,000.